Ecclesial
Movements
and Communities

Abridged Second Edition

Ecclesial
Movements
and Communities
Abridged Second Edition

Brendan Leahy

Ecclesial
Movements
and Communities

Origins, Significance, and Issues

Abridged Second Edition

New City Press
of the Focolare
Hyde Park, New York

Published in the United States by New City Press
202 Comforter Blvd., Hyde Park, NY 12538
www.newcitypress.com
© 2014 Brendan Leahy

Cover design by Durva Correia

Library of Congress Cataloging-in-Publication Data

Leahy, Breandan, 1960-
  Ecclesial movements and communities : origins, significance, and issues / Brendan
Leahy.
      p. cm.
  Includes bibliographical references.
  ISBN 978-1-56548-396-5 (pbk. : alk. paper)
  1. Catholic Church—Societies, etc. 2. Christian communities—Catholic Church. I. Title.
  BX808.L43 2011
  267'.18209045—dc23   2011029494

ISBN 978-1-56548-538-9 (Abridged Second Edition)

Printed in the United States of America

Contents

Appendix

Introduction to First Edition

This book examines the rise of the "new ecclesial movements and communities." Not only are they spiritual resources for the Church, but they are an expression of the Church on the move. In its Directory of International Associations of the Lay Faithful, The Pontifical Council for the Laity provides concise descriptions for over 115 new movements such as the Catholic Charismatic Renewal, Communion and Liberation, the Cursillo, Emmanuel, Focolare, Foyer de Charité, L'Arche, Legion of Mary, the Neocatechumenal Way, Regnum Christi, Sant'Egidio, Schoenstatt and Teams of Our Lady.

While the main and best-known movements were born in Europe, they have spread throughout the world. Many of them, to a greater or lesser extent, are found from North America to Australia, from Brazil to Sweden, from Ireland to Nigeria. Of course, many other movements have been born outside Europe, such as the Couples for Christ Movement, which began in Manila, Philippines; the Holy Trinity Community (Komunitas Tritunggal Mahakudus) founded in Malang, Indonesia; the Secular Missionary Carmel (Carmelo Misionero Seglar) established in Colombia; the Shalom Catholic Community created in Brazil; the Christian Life Movement was founded in Peru and the Madonna House Apostolate was founded in Combermere, Canada.

Specific mention must be made of thousands of ecclesial communities within Charismatic Renewal that, as we shall see again later in the book, began in the United States and spread worldwide. Many of the key communities belong to the Catholic Fraternity of Covenant Communities. Research has indicated that some 100 million people have been touched by the grace of charismatic renewal.

Undoubtedly, the movements demonstrate a great variety in terms of self-understanding and spirituality, external structures and procedures, training or formation methods, goals and fields of work. Yet the overall fact of their presence calls for theological and pastoral consideration. As has been pointed out on several occasions, the newness of the movements has yet to be understood adequately in terms of the positive impact they can have in serving the Kingdom of God at work in today's history.

There have been contrasting views on the significance of ecclesial movements. Some see them as a providential gift of the Holy Spirit to the Church, a way of responding effectively to contemporary challenges. Others, who feel that the movements can arouse suspicion, regard them as a dangerous infection, overthrowing territorial Catholicism and causing a Tridentine form of pastoral care to collapse. For such observers, the movements seem like a providential army that the Roman center will use against the reform of the Church. Yet others consider them to be parallel churches, or unusual cults.

In truth, it is still too close to the emergence of new ecclesial movements in the twentieth century to be able to evaluate them thoroughly. Time is needed to get to know, appreciate and distinguish the distinctive features of each one as well as explore the theological horizons against which to appraise them. This being said, the upcoming fiftieth anniversary of the great Pentecostal event of the Second Vatican Council (1962–1965) offers a golden opportunity to take a look at the presence of new ecclesial movements and communities in the life of the Church in the light of the Council, revisit how they emerged, examine what has been taught about them, explore theological avenues that clarify their relevance and tease out some specific aspects that arise.

There is a further reason why it is timely to explore the topic of ecclesial movements. They are now passing through a period of transition from a more effervescent foundational moment in contact with the founder or original inspiring source, to a subsequent phase of creative fidelity to the original charismatic outpouring. Founders of movements who have died in the past twenty years include Pierre Goursat, co-founder of the Emmanuel Community (1991); Henri Caffarel, founder of Teams of Our Lady (1996); Msgr. Luigi Giussani, founder of Communion and Liberation (2005); Fr. Oreste Benzi, founder of the Comunità Papa Giovanni XXIII Association (2007); Eduardo Bonnin, founder of Cursillos (2008); and Chiara Lubich, founder of the Focolare (2008). Movements are moving into the ordinary rhythm and mission of the Church. This era of transition prompts a deeper recognition, among the movements themselves and in the Church as a whole, of the meaning and contribution ecclesial movements and communities are called to make to the Church and humanity.

Another reason for studying the movements, though not a specific focus of this work, is that some of them manifest spiritual and mystical dimensions worth exploring in the context of theological method, insight and interdisciplinary exchange.

This Book

While acknowledging and occasionally referring to communities and movements in other churches, this book will focus primarily on movements within the Catholic Church, particularly against horizons that emerged from or were suggested by the teachings of the Second Vatican Council.

This book is divided into two sections. (First edition had three sections.) After this introduction and a chapter that defines the nature of ecclesial movements, the first part offers a brief overview of their rise and spread. This section touches on the growing attention afforded them in magisterial teaching and theological reflection, especially in Italy and Germany. The second section presents five theological keys to assist reflection on the phenomenon of movements.

While reference will be made to the literature written about movements in recent years, the specific nature, aim and methods of each individual community merits detailed attention. For more specific information on each movement, its current projects and contact details, readers should visit the individual movements' websites. This book offers a more global treatment of the phenomenon itself rather than a detailed examination of any one movement or community.

Movements and Communities in Our Faith Journey

When speaking about their encounter with the community, members often say it wasn't so much that they met an association or group but rather a Person who changed their lives. For the first time or in a new form, they had an encounter with Jesus Christ. Indeed, in many ways, the expression "baptism in the Spirit" is accurate. For those already baptized, Christianity suddenly came alive for them in a new way. A new window onto the gospel message opened up for them.

The history of the Church is full of such windows opening up. Complementary to the hierarchical-sacramental side of the Christian life, there have been many movements and communities of renewal such as the Benedictines, the Franciscans, the Carmelites and the Vincentians. If readers were to reflect on their own life story, they could recognize how, in their journey following Jesus Christ, they have been influenced, directly or indirectly, by religious orders or associations.

In my own case, I recognize with gratitude how communities born from charisms have been present in my life, some directly, others marginally, but each speaking a word that made a difference for me. I offer this book in grateful recognition of their influence.

By way of conclusion, I'd like to refer to a sentiment expressed by Bernard of Clairvaux (1090–1153) that hits the right note on which to set out. Writing about his religious order and how it related to other movements or orders in his time he commented:

I admire them all. I belong to one of them by observance, but to all of them by charity. We all need one another: the spiritual good which I do not own and possess, I receive from others.... In this exile, the Church is still on pilgrimage and is, in a certain sense, plural: she is a single plurality and a plural unity. All our diversities, which make manifest the richness of God's gifts, will continue to exist in the one house of the Father, which has many rooms. Now there is a division of graces; then there will be distinctions of glory. Unity, both here and there, consists in one and the same charity.

Brendan Leahy

Introduction to Second Edition

This Abridged Second Edition has been prepared especially for the one-day national gathering planned for new ecclesial movements and communities on August 9, 2014 at Our Lady of Good Counsel High School in Olney, Maryland. This event is entitled: *They Were All Gathered Together - A Celebration of Movements & New Communities in the U.S. in Service of the New Evangelization.* It can be seen as part of a much longer sequence of events, beginning with the birth of each of these communities, followed by a number of conferences and gatherings among the movements at various levels.

One of the first and most significant of these gatherings was in St. Peter's Square at the Pentecost vigil of 1998. About 500,000 members of the new ecclesial movements and communities responded to Pope John Paul II's invitation to join him. Four founders of new movements offered their testimonies. Kiko Arguello of the Neocatechumenal Way, Luigi Giussani of Communion and Liberation, and the Canadian founder of L'Arche, Jean Vanier, addressed the Holy Father. Chiara Lubich, foundress of the Focolare Movement, then promised the Pope to strive for communion among the movements and communities within the Church. Speaking on behalf of Charismatic Renewal and all the movements present, Charles Whitehead expressed thanks to the Pope for the gathering.

Patti Gallagher Mansfield of the Catholic Charismatic Renewal addressed Pope Benedict XVI at a similar event in St. Peter's Square just before Pentecost, 2006. Over these years, many U.S. bishops participated in comparable, smaller gatherings on the diocesan level.

In 2008, Bishop Sam Jacobs, a long-time member of the Catholic Charismatic Renewal, invited national representatives of several movements to consider a possible collaboration on a national scale. Cursillo, Focolare, the Neocatechumenal Way, and Worldwide Marriage Encounter all immediately responded positively. Others joined them over the years, participating in conference calls and personal meetings. This group was ultimately called, "Catholic Ecclesial Movements and New Communities in the U.S. in Conversation." It has held receptions, a luncheon, and a workshop for U.S. bishops during their November meetings in Baltimore each year.

The main purpose of this "Conversation" has been twofold: first, to foster communion among the movements and new communities, fully respecting the diverse charisms and thrusts of each one. On the basis of this communion, each is encouraged to live and progress on the path along which God has called that particular movement, while also drawing whatever can be helpful from the others. Secondly, this "Conversation" offers these new gifts to the Church in the U.S., placing the light "on the lampstand." As these gifts are welcomed in the Church here, they should contribute substantially to the New Evangelization.

In fact, the new movements and communities have already contributed greatly to the life of the Church in the U.S. For example, more than one million people have benefitted from a Catholic Cursillo weekend. Millions of lives have been impacted by Life in the Spirit seminars and baptism in the Spirit. A Marriage Encounter weekend has enriched the vocations of several million couples and priests in the U.S. More than 30,000 people are currently deeply committed to the Neocatechumenal Way's catechesis in 900 American parishes. This charism has inspired many vocations to the priesthood and consecrated life, now filling seven new seminaries throughout the U.S., not to mention those entering already existing convents and seminaries. The life of all the new movements and ecclesial communities has helped to preserve the vocations of many priests and consecrated persons, as well as generating new ones.

To be in communion with the Church, Pope John Paul II indicated five requirements for these new communities in *Christifidelis Laici* in 1988: the quest for holiness; communion with the Pope, local bishops and the entire Church; contribution to the Church's task of evangelization; profession of orthodox Catholic teaching; and implementation of the gospel by seeking social justice and human dignity. A review of these five "criteria" leads to the conclusion that each new movement or community may emphasize one or more of them. At the same time, it is the communion among the new movements and communities that enables their members to implement all of them.

Through this communion, we can evangelize. "This is how all will know that you are my disciples, if you have love for one another." (Jn 13:35) Living out our particular vocations in communion with others, we will transform society — the family, culture, the media, the economy, politics, education et al. — with the gospel.

May this communion also help us to recognize God's work, prompting us to be immensely grateful for what He has given to us and the whole Church.

It is our hope that this book will enable many to learn more about this important phenomenon for the Church in the U.S. in the 21st Century. It will also give the grassroots membership of our communities the possibility to become more familiar with one another. We encourage readers to study the various websites indicated in the Appendix called Listing of Movements and New Communities at the end of this book. We also include short summaries provided by the following movements: Arise International (Caritas in Veritate International), The Catholic Charismatic Renewal, the Cursillo Movement, the Focolare Movement, the Neocatechumenal Way, and Worldwide Marriage Encounter. May this new edition lead to a greater commitment to our own path of holiness, the communion among us, and the evangelization of society.

References, endnotes, and bibliography that may apply to this Second Abridged Edition can be found in detail in the First Edition.

Catholic Ecclesial Movements and
New Communities in the U.S. in Conversation

1

Defining "Ecclesial Movements"

Defining "ecclesial movement" or "community" is challenging because these realities are, by their nature, on the move; they are dynamic; they don't easily fit into neat categories. While "movement" is used as an umbrella term, some groups prefer "community" or "association." Others feel uncomfortable with any term that seems to restrict the new experience they are living. Clearly, each movement or community has its own distinctive story. The charismatic energies behind the groups flow in different directions. Nevertheless, in order to reflect and provide a general overview, this book will use the term "movement."

"Ecclesial" Movements

What does it mean, then, when the word "ecclesial" is added to "movement"? At the World Congress of Ecclesial Movements and New Communities, sponsored by the Pontifical Council for the Laity in Rome from May 27 to 29, 1998 the then Cardinal Ratzinger provided a concise description that captures the essential features of ecclesial movements. Referring to the Franciscan movement of the thirteenth century as probably providing "the clearest instance of what a movement is," he affirmed:

> [M]ovements generally derive their origin from a charismatic leader and take shape in concrete communities, inspired by the life of their founder; they attempt to live the Gospel anew, in its totality, and recognize the Church without hesitation as the ground of their life without which they could not exist.

According to this definition, movements are linked to "charisms" that are communicative in the sense that others are attracted by what the charismatic leader is doing and promoting, saying and writing. This, in turn, leads to a spiritual affinity between persons which develops into friendships based on the

15

gospel. Eventually, movements are examined and officially recognized by authorities in the Church first at the local diocesan level and then by the competent office in Rome. In the light of their approval by the Church, they can offer themselves as forms or reflections of the one Church.

The term "ecclesial movement" is general enough to cover a wealth of forms produced by the life-giving creativity of the Spirit. Moving on from that first snapshot provided by Cardinal Ratzinger, it is possible to expand the definition by introducing other elements common among ecclesial movements. In his message to the 1998 World Congress of Movements, John Paul II underlined the dimensions of a common faith journey, communion, as well as the missionary witness associated with new communities that come to life around a charism:

> The originality of the particular charism that gives life to a movement neither claims, nor could claim, to add anything to the richness of the depositum fidei [deposit of the faith]....
> Nevertheless, it represents a powerful support, a moving and convincing reminder to live the Christian experience to the full, with intelligence and creativity.... In this light, the charisms recognized by the Church are ways of deepening one's knowledge of Christ and giving oneself more generously to him, while at the same time rooting oneself ever more deeply in communion with the entire Christian people.

"Ecclesial" is used in reference to movements because it indicates one of the principal original features associated with the communities that have arisen in recent decades. While these movements are made up mostly of lay people, they also include bishops, priests and religious. In so doing, they reflect the whole Church. Accordingly, in affirming that "the Church herself is a movement" John Paul II implied the movements are expressions of the Church in movement.

So it is not quite accurate to refer to many of the new movements and communities in the Church as "lay movements." As Charles Whitehead, one of the leaders of Charismatic Renewal puts it:

They are for the whole Church.... The movements and new communities are truly the Church, in the sense of the community of the baptized which we find in the New Testament and in *Lumen Gentium(LG)*, and therefore the description "ecclesial movements" is more appropriate than "lay movements."

No definition would be complete without underscoring the dynamic element of each movement's commitment to finding itself outside itself in the order of love—that is, in missionary outreach. In his message to the Second World Congress of the Ecclesial Movements and New Communities (Rocca di Papa, May 31 to June 2, 2006), Benedict XVI gave expression to this missionary desire that animates them:

Bring Christ's light to all the social and cultural milieu in which you live. Missionary zeal is proof of a radical experience of ever-renewed fidelity to one's charism that surpasses any kind of weary or selfish withdrawal.... The extraordinary fusion between love of God and love of neighbor makes life beautiful and causes the desert in which we often find ourselves living to blossom anew. Where love is expressed as a passion for the life and destiny of others, where love shines forth in affection and in work and becomes a force for the construction of a more just social order, there the civilization is built.... Become builders of a better world according to the order of love in which the beauty of human life is expressed.

Ecclesial Movements exhibit a variety of initiatives in the social field. The Community of Sant'Egidio is well known for its peace initiatives in places such as Mozambique, Algeria and the Balkans. The Focolare Movement has launched a project entitled "Economy of Communion," promoting a new economic model in the light of the gospel. It is also involved in many nongovernmental social projects around the world. The Teams of Our Lady work to build up healthy marriages. The Communion and Liberation movement organizes many cultural events such as its large annual meeting in Rimini, Italy.

In L'Arche communities, people with and without disabilities share their lives together, giving witness to the reality that persons with disabilities possess inherent qualities of welcome and wonderment, spirituality and friendship. These communities came to life in 1964 through the initiative of Jean Vanier, son of the Governor General of Canada.

Elements of Ecclesial Movements

Movements can be categorized in a number of ways. For instance, in his recent work, *A New Wine and Fresh Skins*, Australian bishop Julian Porteous offers the following categories as a guide to the different characteristics of movements: a) movements that developed before the Second Vatican Council; b) new movements that emerged after the Council; c) communities founded by clerics, priests or religious; d) communities founded by lay people; e) movements that have taken the form of religious life. He also sees the two other defining features of the movements as a) apostolic activity and b) countries and cultures of origin.

The German canon lawyer Christoph Hegge proposes five features that need to be kept in mind in defining ecclesial movements:

1. A unique charism of a founder who is at the center and whose personal vocation attracts others to an experience of conversion to the gospel. Encounter with the charism leads to a radical renewal of one's baptism and a desire to live a collective spirituality.

2. The group that comes to life through the charism is composed of all categories of the faithful.

3. While all members are linked through the charism and its spirituality, the institutional structure of movements is elastic and flexible enough to allow for a variety of ways of belonging to the community.

4. The experience of a structural communion among people of all vocations brought about by a shared charism opens up a renewed understanding of the Church's pastoral, apostolic and evangelizing mission.

5. Ecclesial movements and communities manifest the uni-
   versality or catholicity of the faith. This is so, not so much
   in terms of internationality – though that is very much the
   case – but rather in the sense of the "universal relevancy of
   the message of Christ."

Part 1

The Emergence of Ecclesial Movements

Part 1 of the book will trace the history of the emergence of the movements. Undoubtedly, the Second Vatican Council was a key event along the journey but many developments before the Council were important in paving the way for their recognition. The post-conciliar period is particularly significant for clarifying the place of the movements and providing criteria for evaluating their authenticity.

This section, which covers 100 years or so of history, offers a necessarily relatively brief treatment. Nevertheless, tracing the emergence of movements is stimulating not least because it means noting the interplay of circumstances and key personalities, doctrinal developments and needs of the Church, all of which, from a faith perspective, form a history guided by the Holy Spirit.

2

Arising in the Century of the Church

In the 1920s, two prominent theologians — the Catholic Romano Guardini and the Evangelical Lutheran Otto Dibelius — spoke of the twentieth century as an era when the Church would re-awaken in people. The movements express the realization of that prophecy. Perhaps it was necessary to wait until the twentieth century, the century of the re-awakening of the Church in souls, "to see such a blossoming and variety of autonomous lay movements in the Church, some of which may indeed take their orientation from great charisms of the past but most of which have emerged from new, independent inspirations of the Holy Spirit." This chapter reviews the beginnings of the emergence of ecclesial movements, covering the period up to the Second Vatican Council.

Remote Preparation in the Nineteenth Century

It is important to note that in the twentieth century ecclesial movements did not appear on the ecclesial horizon totally out of the blue. The previous century witnessed many socio-political developments that challenged the Church's self-understanding of identity and mission. The resulting theological and ecclesiological renewal laid the foundation for the arrival of ecclesial movements.

The nineteenth century renewal revolved around a rediscovery of the "mystery" dimension of the Church, a marked contrast with what had gone before. Although generalizations can be suspect, it is nevertheless commonly accepted that the primary model of Church, predominant from the Council of Trent (1545–1563) to the twentieth century, emphasized its hierarchical, sacramental and institutional elements. Several socio-religious factors that need not be explored at this point account for this emphasis. It is important to note, however, that the turning point in Western culture which accompanied the French Revolution also left a deep

23

mark on the Church. Sensing the need to focus once again on the living, organic side of the Church, people began to seek ways of understanding it "internally." Robert Bellarmine (1542–1621) had portrayed the Church as a "perfect society," that had the instruments and structures needed to communicate salvation. But now a realization grew that something more was needed. Re-reading the Church Fathers opened up a discovery of the deeper "mystery" side of the Church.

Encouraged by Leo XIII (1878–1903), during the nineteenth century were founded many social and welfare organizations and associations, such as the St. Vincent de Paul Conferences established by Frédéric Ozanam (1813–1853) and the German social work association set up by Adolph Kolping (1813–1865).

Developments in the Early Twentieth Century

At the beginning of the twentieth century, one that would be marked by two world wars and great historical changes, a new awareness began to grow among lay faithful of their ecclesial vocation, that is, their participation in the mission of the Church as the Body of Christ. In 1917 the Catholic Church's Code of Canon Law gathered its various legal texts into a single document. The third part of book II of this revised Code, "The Laity," provided for associations of the faithful. It recognized three kinds of associations that corresponded to the goals of pursuing spiritual perfection, fostering works of piety or charity, and promoting worship: secular third orders, which promote Christian perfection according to the spirituality of the parent order to which they were associated; confraternities concerned with promoting worship and piety, such as the confraternities of the Sacred Heart, the Blessed Sacrament, the Brown Scapular, the Rosary, and other similar groups; and pious unions, whose purpose was works of charity or piety.

After the 1917 Code's promulgation, many ecclesiastical associations were erected. Catholic Action grew. Secular institutes began to emerge. And a Theology of the laity also began to come to life.

In his memoirs, the former bishop of Sault Ste. Marie, Ontario (Canada), Alex Carter (1909–2002) narrates an episode that reveals the growing recognition of the need to rediscover the role of laity and the lay dimension of the Church. As a young student in Rome, shortly before Pius XI died, Carter attended a papal audience that included a group of Canadian students. He recalls hearing a concise, powerful, and "very prophetic" address, in which the Pope described the Church, the mystical body of Christ, as having become somewhat monstrous, with an enormous head but a shrunken body. Pius XI urged the students to ask lay people to become, with them, witnesses of Christ, bringing Christ back into the workplaces and into the marketplaces.

In 1943, Pius XII's *Mystici Corporis* highlighted the organic nature of the Church. This important encyclical paved the way for the ecclesiology of Vatican II. In it, the Pope developed the Pauline notion of the Church as the Body of Christ with Christ the head and the Church a mystical body. He writes:

> The true meaning of the word "mystical," therefore, reminds us that the Church ... does not consist merely of social and juridical elements nor rest solely on such grounds.... That which raises the Christian society to a level utterly surpassing any order of nature is the Spirit of our Redeemer, the source of all graces, gifts, and miraculous powers, perennially and intimately pervading the Church and acting on her.

Secular institutes offered a more specific form of consecration for men and women who lived out the evangelical counsels in the world, though without public vows. Pius XII recognized the phenomenon of secular institutes, and in 1947 dedicated his letter *Provida Mater Ecclesia* to them.

The work of Yves Congar (1904–1995) on the laity, *Jalons pur une théologie du laïcat* (1953), marked another significant step in recognizing ecclesial movements.

... During the period following World War II up to Vatican II, the theology of the People of God emerged strongly. Based on a rich biblical notion, it undergirded a new sacramental understanding of the Church, emphasizing the common priesthood of all the baptized. The revival of biblical and patristic studies at this time also generated a new look at the notion of catholicity, the Church's unity in diversity, and the image of the Church as communion. Further developments included, in October 1951, the First World Congress for the Lay Apostolate, in Rome. Forty delegates from sixteen countries met to discuss the possibility of forming a world federation. A Second Congress for the Lay Apostolate was held in 1957.

New Associations of Lay Faithful

A number of new associations came to life during the first half of the twentieth century. Gradually, it became clear that they functioned primarily as spiritual networks with three distinguishing characteristics:

a) They had a strong sense of originating in a charism of foundation in which others associated with the founder participated freely and flexibly. For instance, Frank Duff (1889–1980) founded the Legion of Mary in Dublin during a period of great poverty, just at the time of Irish independence. Believing in the call of all the baptized to holiness, his movement promoted spiritual development and advancing the kingdom of Christ through Mary.

During World War II, the Focolare Movement came to life in Italy around Chiara Lubich (1920–2008). Discovering the gospel as a code of life that could be lived from the perspective of unity and fraternity, she and her followers sought to bring Jesus' art of loving into all aspects of their lives, thereby renewing relationships at all levels around them and so contributing to the realization of Jesus' last will and testament: "may they all be one" (Jn 17:21).

The Cursillo Movement also began in the context of World War II around Eduardo Bonnin (1917–2008). At a time when religion was being more and more marginalized in Spain, the Young Men's Catholic Action began to plan a large-scale pilgrimage in 1948 to Compostela.

In Canada the Madonna House apostolate's "little mandate" of love developed around Catherine de Hueck Doherty (1896–1985). Having lived through various personal traumas, Catherine's strong social concern and spiritual intuitions of the Christian East (she grew up in Russia) gave life to a community of lay men and women as well as priests who all sought to live the revolution of love based on the life of a Christian family: the life of Nazareth.

b) These new associations were made up of people of all vocations and walks of life—lay, celibate and married, priests, religious, young and old—with a wide variety of forms of commitment, something quite new before Vatican II.

In the aftermath of World War II, a young Jesuit, Riccardo Lombardi (1908–1979), became convinced that the time had come for terms like "brotherhood" and "sisterhood" to take their place beside "equality" and "freedom." On February 10, 1952, Pius XII officially approved the group that developed around Lombardi as "The Movement for a Better World."

c) A third feature that distinguished the pre-conciliar era was an interest among new groups in renewing ecclesial life itself as well as bearing witness and spreading the gospel. At a time when the Church, especially in Europe, was seeing the rise of systematic or practical atheism, these new movements were providing fresh energy.

In the early 1950s, realizing the need to rebuild the Christian presence in the student world, Father Luigi Giussani (1922–2005), a professor at the Theological Faculty near Milan, decided to give up his academic post and dedicate himself to teaching religion in schools. The small group of students that soon gathered around him led to the establishment of the Student Youth Movement. The Archbishop of Milan at that time, Giovanni Battista Montini, who became Pope Paul VI, encouraged this new movement. Soon it involved undergraduates and adults.

During this period of growth the movements were subjected to study and scrutiny. Time was needed to clarify their place in the Church, and the Second Vatican Council played an important part in bringing about that clarification.

3

Setting Important Parameters:
The Movements and Vatican II

In his work on the Second Vatican Council, John W. O'Malley remarks that "the best — indeed, the indispensable — approach to understanding Roman Catholicism today is through Vatican II." The Council, a true event of the Spirit, continues to guide the Catholic Church's journey. It provides a magisterial and theological compass, as well as serving as the "essential and fundamental Magna Charta" of the Church today. Though the Council did not deal specifically with ecclesial movements, conciliar doctrine became crucial to recognizing their place in the Church. The Council's "hermeneutic of reform," as Benedict XVI puts it, provided a multi-faceted framework for reading and receiving the new ecclesial communities.

Research needs to be done on how the existence of movements impacted the Council. Nevertheless, the canonist Gianfranco Ghirlanda has remarked that they were moving in directions being pointed out by the Spirit, and so the Council assembly, as an event of the same Spirit, "could not but make its own these directions." Indeed, lay men and women such as Frank Duff, the Irish founder of the Legion of Mary, James Norris, the American activist known for his work with refugees, and the Australian theologian Rosemary Goldie, a member of the Permanent Committee for International Congresses of the Lay Apostolate, were invited as auditors to the Council.

The Dominican theologian Yves Congar played an active role in formulating the conciliar texts. He explains, "Something happened at the Council and the dominant values in our way of looking at the Church were changed by the Council." In order to place the Church in a better position in the world so as to communicate God in modern times, the Council undertook a thorough review of its identity and mission. Its theological, canonical, and pastoral perspectives became relevant in understanding ecclesial

movements; just so, the movements themselves became important in interpreting the Council.

Mystery-Communion-Mission

The Council endorsed the notion of associations of the faithful: "The most holy council earnestly recommends these associations, which surely answer the needs of the apostolate of
the Church among many peoples and countries…. Among these
associations, moreover, international associations or groups of
Catholics must be specially appreciated at the present time." But
of greater significance for ecclesial movements was its proposal
that the Church be renewed through the rediscovery of the three
themes that run through Council documents: mystery, communion and mission. The Council proposed a vision of the Church
as icon of the Trinity.

The Church is Mystery. The Council underscored the
"mystery" dimension of the Church. It affirmed that, in a way
analogous to its founder and Lord Jesus Christ, the Church is a
human-divine reality. Since it is founded and rooted in the plan
of God who revealed himself eschatologically in history through
Jesus Christ, then what should emerge most is the divine plan of
salvation, not the figure of a Church made up of detached structures, ministries and powers:

> [T]he society structured with hierarchical organs and the
> Mystical Body of Christ, are not to be considered as two
> realities, nor are the visible assembly and the spiritual com-
> munity, nor the earthly Church and the Church enriched
> with heavenly things; rather they form one complex reality
> which coalesces from a divine and a human element. For this
> reason, by no weak analogy, it is compared to the mystery
> of the incarnate Word. As the assumed nature inseparably
> united to Him, serves the divine Word as a living organ of
> salvation, so, in a similar way, does the visible social struc-
> ture of the Church serve the Spirit of Christ, who vivifies it,
> in the building up of the body (see *Eph.* 4:16).

The Church is Communion. From the key conciliar notion of
Church as Mystery emerges another—Church as Communion.
Indeed, it has been declared authoritatively that the ecclesiology

of communion is *the* key ecclesiological idea of Vatican II. The opening statement of the constitution on the Church affirms the communitarian sense of the Church gathered around the Crucified and Risen Christ:

> Christ is the light of the nations.... Since the Church is in Christ like a sacrament or as a sign and instrument both of a very closely knit union with God and of the unity of the whole human race, it desires now to unfold more fully to the faithful of the Church and to the whole world its own inner nature and universal mission.

Twenty years after the Council, in his apostolic exhortation on the Laity, *Christifideles Laici*, John Paul II summarized the Council's teaching in this regard. He describes the Council's vision of the unity, distinction, and mutual relations in the Church-communion among the three fundamental states of life of the People of God: laity, ordained ministry and religious life. They are different yet complementary, in a dynamic relationship to one another.

The Church is Mission. The third major theme that characterizes the purpose of the Church is mission. The Council's deep yearning for the evangelization of the contemporary world, though not made as explicit as it might have been, culminates in the missionary decree *Ad Gentes*. In it the Council defines evangelization as "that activity through which, in obedience to Christ's command and moved by the grace and love of the Holy Spirit, the Church makes itself fully present to all persons and peoples in order to lead them to the faith, freedom and peace of Christ by example of its life and teaching, and also by the sacraments and other means of grace."

Universal sharing in the mission of Jesus Christ. Taking up the theology of the triple office of prophet, king and priest that Pius XII had applied to Christ, the Council teaches that because the whole people of God is united to Jesus Christ through faith and baptism, in the Holy Spirit it shares—albeit in different ways—in the priestly, prophetic and royal mission of Christ (see 1 Pet 1:9–10).

Sent out to the whole world. In the power of the Holy Spirit, the risen Christ, who lives in the midst of his disciples to the end of time, sends the Church out to share the gift it has received (see Mt 18:20; 28:19–20).

Parameters for Ecclesial Movements

These three broad themes opened up important parameters for understanding ecclesial movements. Some of them can be mentioned here briefly.

First, the Council widens the notion of lay apostolate by rooting it in the baptismal identity and mission of every Christian. All the baptized, lay and ordained, are brothers and sisters in the one common project of building up the family of humankind for which Jesus gave his life.

Second, by underlining the universal call to holiness the Council opens the way for greater communion among all the baptized—lay, religious or ordained. It calls them to live out together their essential baptismal vocation to holiness, recognizing their equal dignity as Christians in a communion that extends beyond the visible confines of the Church.

Third, in presenting a dynamic sense of revelation and God's continuing dialogue with the Church, the Council underlines the Holy Spirit's role in the ever-deeper penetration of the gospel along the Church's journey, through charisms and spiritual experience.

Fourth, the Church's rediscovery of its charismatic dimension has paved the way for understanding the place of movements in the Church. John O'Malley points out that the notion of "charism" was part of the Council's new lexicon, indeed one of the "interiority-words" that marked it. "Charism" was clearly something new.

Lumen Gentium, n.12, contains the main text on the place of charisms. It states that the Holy Spirit sanctifies and leads the People of God not only through sacraments and ordained ministries but also through charisms, be they be extraordinary or ordinary.

This passage, among others, became a key text for interpreting the interplay among the Church's charismatic and institutional dimensions and the movements viewed as an expression of the charismatic gifts. This topic will be revisited in the section that reviews the 1998 meeting of the movements with John Paul II.

4

Encouraging, Clarifying, Providing Criteria: From the Second Vatican Council to the 1987 Synod on the Laity

The Second Vatican Council set the stage for movements to be recognized, indeed to multiply. In the new atmosphere that followed the Council, lay and ordained Catholics alike felt an increasing need to form free and spontaneous groups in which they could deepen their Christian life together and exercise effective Christian witness. Movements that had caused perplexity during the 1950s were approved. Many others came to life.

The Neocatechumenal Way is an example of a new movement (although its members prefer the expression "Way") that came to life after the Council.

Another movement that emerged in the late 1960s and early 1970s is the Community of Sant'Egidio Its three pillars are prayer, communicating the gospel and friendship with the poor.

The Communion and Liberation movement emerged before the Council, but its first "fraternity groups" were set up in the latter half of the 1970s. Soon the Fraternity of Communion and Liberation spread from Italy to other countries; this diffusion led to the establishment of Communion and Liberation.

Encouraging, Directing, Instructing — Pope Paul VI and Movements

The popes that followed the Council provided strong support for the movements. The first of the post-conciliar popes, the saintly Paul VI (1963–1978), assumed the unenviable task of steering the Bark of the Church in turbulent times. In 1970, summarizing the aim of the Council, he wrote, "It wanted to create an atmosphere of collective and mutual pastoral (outreach). It wanted to strengthen the working bonds of love that unite us all in Christ. It wanted to give to the Church in its modern structures — enthusiasm, solidarity, the liveliness of the early Christian community. If we were to use advertising language we could say the Council wanted to be 'operation heart.'"

It was this "operation heart" that the new communities and movements seemed to encapsulate. Pope Paul VI encouraged this:

> Newness seems the characteristic promise of the Council: spiritual re-awakening, aggiornamento, easy and happy ecumenism, a new expression of Christianity according to the needs of our times, the reform of the law and laws of the Church.... A vision of newness, youthfulness, courage, happiness, peace — this is what the Council proposed to the Church.... Let's desire, yes, and let's work to give the post-Conciliar Church a new face! Above all an interior renewal.

As the new life of movements began to manifest itself, Pope Paul VI encouraged recognition of the contribution of new movements and communities to the Church through numerous meetings and addresses, and by approving their statutes Chiara Lubich, founder of the Focolare Movement, said that Paul VI had provided her movement with a "precious legacy of encouragement, direction and instruction" that would always remain alive. In 1973 he assigned to the Pontifical Council for Laity the official Vatican responsibility for ecclesial movements.

The Charismatic Dimension Rediscovered — Pope John Paul II and Movements

Pope John Paul II (1978–2005) offered unprecedented support in promoting the role of movements in the life of the Church. Continuing Pope Paul VI's positive approach, he acknowledged these new communities as providential fruits of the action of the Holy Spirit and bearers of renewal for the Church's apostolic life and mission. For him they were clearly linked with the Second Vatican Council and the "new Pentecost" that Pope John XXIII so desired. From the beginning of his pontificate he made a point of meeting with movements.

> I followed their work attentively, accompanying them with prayer and constant encouragement. From the beginning of

my Pontificate, I have given special importance to the progress of ecclesial movements, and I have had the opportunity to appreciate the results of their widespread and growing presence during my pastoral visits to parishes and my apostolic journeys. I have noticed with pleasure their willingness to devote their energies to the service of the See of Peter and the local Churches. I have been able to point to them as something new that is still waiting to be properly accepted and appreciated.

The movements and communities frequently experienced John Paul II's warm and encouraging support, most evident at the milestone 1998 Pentecost meeting of movements at St. Peter's Square. In numerous other audiences and meetings, letters, visits and lunches, he cultivated vibrant relationships with the founders, leaders and members of the new movements.

John Paul II's theology was shaped by the Second Vatican Council. This perhaps explains his appreciation of movements as an expression of the charismatic principle. It is also evident, however, that he understood the charismatic principle in the light of his own deeply personal awareness of the role of the Spirit in the life of the Church and humanity. For instance, in his encyclical on the Holy Spirit, *Dominum et vivificantem*, he reiterated the Second Vatican Council's affirmation that the Church "is in Christ like a sacrament or as a sign or instrument both of a very closely knit union with God and of the unity of the whole human race."

John Paul II develops this notion in reference to the event of Christ with its supreme gift of the Spirit: "As a sacrament, the Church is a development from the Paschal Mystery of Christ's 'departure,' living by his ever new 'coming' by the power of the Holy Spirit, within the same mission of the Paraclete — Spirit of truth. Precisely this is the essential mystery of the Church, as the Council professes."

Accordingly, John Paul II also affirms that "while it is an historical fact that the Church came forth from the Upper Room on the day of Pentecost," in a certain sense "one can say that she has never left it. Spiritually, the event of Pentecost does not belong only to the past: the Church is always in the Upper Room that she bears in her heart." In this sense, he understood the Church to be in an ever new situation of Pentecost.

Discerning the Movements with Criteria of Ecclesiality

The Council generated an extensive body of theological literature on the topic of charism. Well-known authors such as Karl Rahner, Hans Urs von Balthasar and Avery Dulles reflected on the theme, which exploded into life through the charismatic renewal, and was reinforced through the theology of ministry.

The International Catholic Charismatic Renewal emerged two years after the close of Vatican II. At Pentecost, during the Holy Year of 1975, 10,000 people came to Rome from all parts of the world for the International Congress of the Charismatic Renewal. Many of the charismatic renewal groups became covenant communities. The experience of a Charismatic Renewal prayer group, for instance, led Pierre Goursat (1914–1991) and Martine Laffitte-Catta to found the Emmanuel Community, in Paris.

By 1982 Francis Sullivan was able to write that "the words 'charism' and 'charismatic' are in such common use among Catholics today that it is hard to realize that they were so unfamiliar to most of us less than twenty years ago." In 1985, for example, Avery Dulles commented, "In grappling with the interplay of the institutional and the charismatic ... we shall be dealing with one of the most crucial problem-areas in ecclesiology."

From the 1960s onward the Charismatic Renewal continued to grow. As early as 1976 Cardinal Leon Josef Suenens interpreted Charismatic Renewal as a movement of the Spirit offered to the entire Church and destined to rejuvenate every part of the Church's life. By the early 2000s, more than 120 million Catholics worldwide had become linked to the Catholic Charismatic Renewal.

By the 1980s, many other new ecclesial movements were becoming increasingly evident in different forums of church life. Increasingly, it became clear that ecclesial movements deserved more articulate theological and pastoral consideration. The birth and spread of the movements had certainly brought unexpected newness, but this innovation struck some as disruptive, giving rise to questions, uneasiness and tensions. Such growth and change generated inevitable frictions, in which different sides were at fault in different ways.

A first international meeting of movements was held in Rome from September 23 to 27, 1981, and a second near Rome, in Rocca di Papa, from February 28 to March 4, 1987. More and more literature began to be published on the theological rationale of ecclesial movements, including both positive and negative pastoral assessments.

This period of tension, with prejudices and reservations being expressed, tested the movements' fidelity and verified their charisms. Against this background of positive and negative appraisal, a lively discussion concerning movements took place during the 1987 Synod of Bishops on the Laity. This particular synod was remarkable in that it offered lay leaders of movements an opportunity to address the gathered bishops.

In *Christifideles Laici,* the document that the Synod produced, quoting both Vatican II and Canon Law, Pope John Paul II embraced the enthusiasm as well as the reservations expressed. Beginning the Apostolic Exhortation, he notes how "the Holy Spirit continues to renew the youth of the Church" and how "he has inspired new aspirations towards holiness and the participation of so many lay faithful. This is witnessed, among other ways, in ... the flourishing of groups, associations and spiritual movements" (n. 2). Later in the same document he comments:

> In some ways lay associations have always been present throughout the Church's history as various confraternities, third orders and sodalities testify even today. However, in modern times such lay groups have received a special stimulus, resulting in the birth and spread of a multiplicity of group forms: associations, groups, communities, movements. We can speak of a *new era of group endeavors* of the lay faithful. (N. 29)

However, although the Second Vatican Council's ecclesiology of communion clearly expresses the "right" to form lay associations, the Pope affirms the need to formulate "criteria" for discerning the authenticity of the forms which such groups take in the Church. After all, the Church is a "sign and instrument of unity."

The Pope, therefore, proposes "criteria for ecclesiality" to discern the authenticity of the forms that such groups take in the Church's communion. *First*, the community or movement should be an instrument leading people to holiness in the Church. *Second*, each movement should be a forum where the Catholic faith as the Church interprets it is professed responsibly. *Third*, each community should be in a strong and authentic communion with the Pope and with the local bishop in the local church. They should be willing to work together with others. *Fourth*, movements should take as their own the Church's missionary goals of evangelization, sanctification of humankind and the Christian formation of people's conscience in order to spread the Gospel into all walks of life. *Fifth*, the movements should exhibit a *commitment to being present in human society* so as to bring about more just and loving conditions. The movements demonstrate their success in meeting these criteria by the fruits they show in their organizational life and in their works.

These criteria have proven important in evaluating new communities and movements. In *Vita consecrata*, the post-synodal Apostolic Exhortation on the Consecrated Life and its Mission in the Church and in the World (March 25, 1996, n. 62), John Paul II repeats that while there is reason to rejoice at the Holy Spirit's action in bringing new communities to life, there is also a need for discernment regarding these charisms.

Cardinal L. J. Suenens

This discussion would not be complete without referring to a major figure in the story of Vatican II and charisms, before, during and after the Council. Through his encouragement and his writings, Cardinal Suenens (1904–1996) contributed much to a new understanding of movements and communities. Suenens saw that charisms were not a mere "peripheral or accidental phenomenon in the life of the Church," but belonging to the very nature of the Church and so "of vital importance for the building up of the mystical body." He contended that Church always contains charisms, both the ordinary and the extraordinary. Accordingly, he proposed that they receive greater emphasis in the Council's treatment of the Church as the People of God.

5

A Significant Milestone — Pentecost 1998

John Paul II guided preparations for the 2000 Jubilee Millennium celebrations with keen interest. He saw the turn of the twentieth century as a time to live "a new Advent." From the beginning of his papacy, he set his gaze on the entrance of the Church into the third millennium. In his 1994 apostolic letter, *Tertio Millennio Adveniente*, he proposed dedicating the three years preceding the Jubilee to the Trinity, focusing 1997 on Christ, 1998 on the Spirit and 1999 on the Father.

In his 1996 homily at the Vigil of Pentecost, John Paul II inaugurated preparations for the Jubilee Year. In that address, the Pope once again spoke about the ecclesial movements, repeating something he first noted in 1984: "They are a sign of the freedom of forms in which the one Church is realized and they represent a sure novelty that still needs to be adequately understood in its positive efficacy for the Kingdom of God working today in history."

Concerning Jubilee celebrations, he said that during 1998, the year dedicated to the Holy Spirit, he would be counting especially on the "common witness and collaboration of the movements." This came to pass on May 31, 1998, when over 300,000 members of movements and ecclesial communities gathered in St. Peter's Square.

The 1998 Pentecost Meeting — A Decisive Turning Point

Cardinal Rylko, who later became president of the Pontifical Council for the Laity, described the iconic gathering of movements with the Pope on Pentecost 1998 as a "decisive turning point for the life and mission of movements and communities." Four founders of new movements offered their testimonies to the Pope and to the packed St. Peter's Square: Chiara Lubich of the Focolare, Msgr. Luigi Giussani of Communion and Liberation, Kiko Argüello of the Neocatechumenal Way and Jean Vanier of

L'Arche. Speaking on behalf of Charismatic Renewal and all the movements present, Charles Whitehead expressed thanks to the Pope for the gathering.

As the Pope himself noted, this "truly unprecedented" event was the first time these movements and communities had gathered together with the pontiff. Although he himself had met with movements one by one, Pentecost 1998 allowed him to encounter them all together, and the movements to encounter each other. In his address, he framed his reflection in terms of the Pentecost experience and the Second Vatican Council's rediscovery of the charismatic dimension in the Church:

> The institutional and charismatic aspects are co-essential as it were to the Church's constitution. They contribute, although differently, to the life, renewal and sanctification of God's People. It is from this providential rediscovery of the Church's charismatic dimension that, before and after the Council, a remarkable pattern of growth has been established for ecclesial movements and new communities.

John Paul II also called attention to "a new stage" unfolding for the movements — ecclesial maturity. He invited them to bring forth the more "mature" fruits of communion and commitment that "the Church expects from you." He explained his own passionate commitment to the movements:

> In our world, often dominated by a secularized culture which encourages and promotes models of life without God, the faith of many is sorely tested, and is frequently stifled and dies. Thus we see an urgent need for powerful proclamation and solid, in-depth Christian formation. There is so much need today for mature Christian personalities, conscious of their baptismal identity, of their vocation and mission in the Church and in the world! There is great need for living Christian communities! And here are the movements and the new ecclesial communities: they are the response, given by the Holy Spirit, this providential response.

Reminding those gathered at St. Peter's Square of the role that competent ecclesiastical authorities have in discernment, he concluded with a rousing mandate:

Today, from this upper room in St. Peter's Square, a great prayer rises: Come, Holy Spirit, come and renew the face of the earth.... Come, Holy Spirit, and make ever more fruitful the charisms that you have bestowed on us.... Today from this square, Christ says to each of you: "Go into all the world and preach the gospel to the whole creation" (Mk 16:15). He is counting on every one of you, and so is the Church. "Lo," the Lord promises, "I am with you always to the close of the age" (Mt 28:20).

The World Congress

During the three days preceding the Pentecost Vigil, 350 delegates from around the world, representing 54 movements and new communities as well as observers from other churches, met in Rome. Cardinal Stafford, who at that time was president of the Council for the Laity, commented that it "surpassed expectations," adding "there was something very special about the week." The movements' character emerged as "particular events" arising from the Holy Spirit who, as the agent of the new evangelization, inspires the actual forms of the Church's missionary activity.

In his message to the congress, John Paul II referred to the movements as one of "the most significant fruits of that springtime in the Church which was foretold by the Second Vatican Council." It was encouraging, he said, to see how "this springtime is advancing and revealing the freshness of the Christian experience based on personal encounter with Christ." He stressed again unity between the institutional and the charismatic dimensions of the Church: "Both are co-essential to the divine constitution of the Church founded by Jesus, because they both help to make the mystery of Christ and his saving work present in the world. Together they aim to renew, each in its own way, the self-awareness of the Church, which in a certain sense may be called a 'movement.'"

A Significant Church Event

A priest who took part, Silvano Cola, noted, "Perhaps it will take years to realize the full importance of Pentecost '98." Certainly the comments of many participants reflect their appreciation of the magnitude and significance of the event. Oreste Pesari, executive director of the International Catholic Charismatic Renewal, commented: "I believe that the first gift we received was that of feeling at home, feeling we are fully Church. Not that we were not so before, but now there is a new awareness of this in us and in others." He and many others felt that God had bestowed a gift that participants could bring to the whole Church. "Over and above how things will work out concretely," Pesari evaluated, "this Pentecost meeting has been a new outpouring of the Holy Spirit, a new joy, a new life. I believe that the Church of the third millennium has really begun." According to the chaplain of the European Cursillo Movement, "This event has been a confirmation for us of our belonging to the Church. It has prompted us further to go and evangelize the world around us. It was great getting to know the other movements. Now we will work even more in communion with the other realities of the Church. The power of mission lies in communion."

Luigi Giussani, founder and leader of the Communion and Liberation movement, wrote to his community:

> The encounter with John Paul II was for me the greatest day of our history. It was the "cry" that God gave us as witnesses of unity, of unity of the whole Church ...

Those gathered before the Pope that day could visualize the countenance of the post-Conciliar Church—a people on a journey who, in obedience to her pastors, come to the immense Upper Room of St. Peter's Square in order to listen to 'that voice' and regain strength for the journey. The Pope was happy. 'I count on you,' he said. These words penetrated everyone's heart. It was as if the Scripture reading about Pentecost was becoming incarnate. It was happening also for us."

Growing in Communion

John Paul II's invitation that the movements grow in a more mature communion found willing listeners. The leaders, representatives, and members of the various movements began to explore how they could strengthen even more their relationships of communion with one another. Bishops too nurtured an increased pastoral attention towards the movements. In the following year approximately 200 congresses of movements met locally all over the world. They indicated their willingness to strengthen their communion with one another and in missionary collaboration with their local churches.

In a special follow-up conference organized by the Focolare Movement, the Community of Sant'Egidio and Charismatic Renewal, the founders and leaders of 41 ecclesial movements and new communities met in Speyer, Germany, on June 7–8, 1999. John Paul II sent a letter of encouragement with Bishop Rylko, who at the time was secretary of the Pontifical Council for the Laity.

Also in 1999, a hundred representatives of the world's bishops along with some of the movements' founders gathered for a study seminar to reflect on this "phase two" in the history of the new communities. They reflected on the movements' missionary drive as well as their close link to the Petrine ministry, considering how they could contribute to their local pastoral apostolate and action. In other words, how could the movements bear as much fruit as possible in the local churches?

Concerning the positive incorporation of movements into the parish and into the particular Church, Cardinal Ratzinger commented, "It is not possible simply to give a recipe" for making this happen. While recognizing that each bishop, as head of the Church in his own diocese is the final arbiter, he also acknowledged that "some rules are necessary but then a great deal depends on the persons involved. That is my experience. If the persons—the parish priest, the groups and also the bishops—are amenable, solutions will be found." Bishops must consider the gifts that these movements bring to the Church, but also must "help the movements to find the right road … with the responsibility for peaceful harmony within the Church."

The tone of Cardinal Ratzinger's observations was encouraging, practical and full of wisdom. He advocated attitudes and values that would find an authoritative confirmation in a significant letter that John Paul II issued in early 2001, *Novo Millennio Ineunte* ("At the Beginning of the New Millennium"). The next chapter, then, will discuss how this encouraging approach continued after Cardinal Ratzinger became Pope Benedict XVI

6

Pope Benedict XVI and
Pope Francis on Movements

Pope Benedict and the Movements

J ust one month after his election as Pope, Benedict XVI called for another large gathering of ecclesial movements, signaling his intention to continue his predecessors' encouragement of them. And on June 3, 2006, that gathering took place. This chapter's reflection on Benedict XVI's view of movements needs to begin, however, by acknowledging the "hermeneutic of reform" that emerged during the Second Vatican Council, as it is the lens through which Pope Benedict views in the movements the work of the Risen Christ in the power of the Spirit.

Addressing the Roman Curia on December 21, 2005, the Pope spoke of this hermeneutic as one "of renewal in the continuity of the one subject-Church which the Lord has given to us ... a subject which increases in time and develops, yet always remaining the same, the one subject of the journeying People of God." For Benedict, the ecclesial movements and communities express a key notion from the Second Vatican Council's document on divine revelation, Dei verbum—the People of God's continuous renewal within the continuity of the great Tradition of the Church.

The Pope's Prior Contact with Movements

We have already noted that Pope Benedict speaks to and of movements from his own first-hand experience. As early as the 1960s, when he was a professor at Tübingen, he met with some movements, including the Neocatechumenal Way. His own studies of the Church Fathers convinced him that baptism had become an almost forgotten sacrament. In the Neocatechumenal Way, however, he discovered young people, struck by the discovery of the gospel, participating in a new post-baptismal catechumenate. Journeying together in the adventure of faith, they had re-appropriated their baptism as individuals, and as a community.

Towards the end of the 1960s, in an era marked by Marxist revolutionary spirit, theologians such as Henri De Lubac, Hans Urs von Balthasar, Marie-Joseph Le Guillou and Louis Bouyer, together with Cardinal Ratzinger, had been planning a new theological and cultural review. In Italy Ratzinger met people who had truly understood the Christian revolution—Msgr. Luigi Giussani and the Communion and Liberation movement. This contact led to the establishment and publication of the international Catholic review, *Communio.*

While bishop of Regensburg, through his contact with the Paderborn professor Heribert Mühlen, Ratzinger met the Charismatic Renewal. He noticed how the young Christian members of this movement were energized by the power of the Spirit.

As prefect of the Congregation for the Doctrine of the Faith, Joseph Cardinal Ratzinger was in a privileged position to evaluate the movements' impact. In a 1985 interview he affirmed:

> Every council, in order really to yield fruit, must be followed by a wave of holiness…. What is hopeful … is the rise of new movements which nobody had planned and which nobody has called into being, but which have sprung spontaneously from the inner vitality of the faith itself. What is manifested in them … is something like a pentecost season in the Church…. I find it marvelous that the Spirit is once more stronger than our programs and brings himself into play in an altogether different way than we had imagined…. Our task—the task of the office holders in the Church and of theologians—is to keep the door open to them, to prepare room for them.

Some years later, in another published interview he discussed various difficulties that had arisen regarding the movements. He advised against getting fixated on such problems: "One can always raise objections to individual movements … but whatever else you may say, we can observe innovative things emerging there. In these movements, Christianity is presented as an experience of newness and is suddenly felt by people—who often come from very far outside—as a chance to live in this century."

Before becoming Pope, at the May 1998 World Congress of Movements, Ratzinger made his most significant statement concerning the theological place of movements in the Church. This address will be discussed in the next section of this book.

Approaching the Movements with a Great Deal of Love

Given his long-standing relations with movements, the support and encouragement he gave them after becoming Pope comes as no surprise. In a May 30, 2005 address to the Italian Episcopal Conference, he spoke of the movements' contribution in terms of mission:

> You have also shed light on the need for parishes to assume a more missionary attitude in their daily pastoral work so as to be open to a more intense collaboration with all the living forces available to the Church today. It is very important in this regard to strengthen the communion between the parish structures and the various "charismatic" groups that have sprung up in recent decades and are widespread in Italy, so that the mission can reach out to all the milieus of life.

At the World Youth Day in Cologne (summer 2005), he pointed out the relevancy of movements for young people. Having recommended to the young people gathered there *the Compendium of the Catechism of the Catholic Church*, he noted, "Obviously books alone are not enough. Form communities based on faith! In recent decades, movements and communities have come to birth in which the power of the Gospel is keenly felt. Seek communion in faith, like fellow travelers." He also indicated that "the spontaneity of new communities is important, but it is also important to preserve communion with the Pope and with the bishops. It is they who guarantee that we are … living as God's great family, founded by the Lord through the Twelve Apostles."

Pope Benedict does not discount the difficulties. In a 1997 interview with Peter Seewald, he acknowledges the tensions that can arise.

Benedict sees how ecclesial movements are important for all members of the Church, including bishops. On February 8, 2007, in order to underline the new maturity of communion among movements, the Pope met with bishops close to two movements—the Focolare and the Community of Sant'Egidio. He repeated his conviction that "that the multiplicity and the unity of the charisms and ministries are inseparable in the life of the Church." He continued, "this unity and multiplicity which comprises the People of God in some way also makes itself manifest today, with many bishops being gathered here with the Pope, near to two different Ecclesial Movements, characterized by a strong missionary dimension." He emphasized for bishops the value of involvement in movements: "The communion between bishops and Movements, therefore, provides a valid impulse for a renewed commitment by the Church in announcing and witnessing to the Gospel of hope and charity in every corner of the world."

In an October 18, 2010 letter to seminarians, Benedict XVI describes the movements as "a magnificent thing. You know how much I esteem them and love them as a gift of the Holy Spirit to the Church." In doing so he underlines the importance of mutual acceptance and understanding among the movements in the unity of Christ's Body.

Holiness and the Radicality of the Gospel

Benedict XVI, in a manner reminiscent of his predecessor John Paul II, remains convinced that the movements are a vital source of life within the Church not yet fully discovered. He views them also as movements of holiness. In his May 13, 2010 address to bishops at the Shrine of Our Lady in Fatima, he recalled the words of John Paul II: "The Church needs above all great currents, movements and witnesses of holiness" because "it is from holiness that is born every authentic renewal of the Church ... [and] a renewed form of presence in the heart of human existence and of the culture of nations." He continued,

> One could say, "the Church has need of these great currents, movements and witnesses of holiness ... but there are none!" In this regard, I confess to you the pleasant surprise that I had in making contact with the movements and the new ecclesial communities. Watching them, I had the joy and the grace to see how, at a moment of weariness in the Church, at a time when we were hearing about "the winter of the Church," the Holy Spirit was creating a new springtime, awakening in young people and adults alike the joy of

being Christian, of living in the Church, which is the living Body of Christ. Thanks to their charisms, the radicality of the Gospel, the objective contents of the faith, the living flow of her tradition, are all being communicated in a persuasive way and welcomed as a personal experience, as adherence in freedom to the present event of Christ.

Five months later, in Palermo, he recounted the story of the recently beatified Chiara Luce Badano, who had been a member of a movement. Noting the important role of Chiara Badano's family as a "miniature church," the Pope also pointed out that each miniature church is inserted into the "great Church," that is, into the family of God that Christ came to form. Ecclesial movements and associations are expressions of that great Church. They serve not themselves, but Christ and the Church. They produce fruits of holiness.

Pope Francis and the Movements

From the very beginning of his mission as Bishop of Rome, Pope Francis has met with many leaders and members of new movements and communities. In his Apostolic Letter, *Evangelii Gaudium* (The Joy of the Gospel) he describes their rise and growth "as the work of the Holy Spirit, who blazes new trails" responding to the search for a deep spirituality and a more real sense of belonging in people's lives.

He admits that initially he had reservations about communities such as Charismatic Renewal. He felt they were "some kind of samba school." When he got to know them and see all the good charismatic renewal was doing for the Church, he became an enthusiastic supporter. Indeed he ended up the spiritual assistant for charismatic renewal in Argentina nominated by the Conference of Bishops. It was with great joy, therefore, that he met with 50,000 of the charismatic Renewal in the Olympic Stadium in Rome on June 1, 2014.

In the course of that meeting he defined Charismatic Renewal as "a current of grace in the Church and for the Church" and he indicated the path for them to follow:

"This is your path: evangelization, spiritual ecumenism, caring for the poor and needy, and welcoming the marginalized.

And all of it is based on worship! The foundation of the renewal is worshiping God!"

He advised against too much organization and excessive planning:

> "Go out into the streets and evangelize. Proclaim the Gospel. Remember that the Church was born 'on the move,' that Pentecost morning. Draw close to the poor and touch in their flesh the wounded flesh of Jesus. Let yourselves be guided by the Holy Spirit, in freedom; and please, don't put the Holy Spirit in a cage! Be free!"

Before leaving the gathering, Pope Francis also invited the crowd to St. Peter's Square for Pentecost 2017 to celebrate the 50th anniversary of their movement.

In his meeting in the Vatican with the Neocatechumenal Way on February 1, 2014, Pope Francis thanked its members, especially the families, for all they do for the Church. He also offered recommendations: to take the greatest care to build and preserve the communion within the particular Churches; to pay special attention to the cultural context in which families of the Way work, recognizing that the Spirit is always at work in all contexts; to take loving care of one another, especially the weakest, respecting each individual's freedom to choose their way of living out their faith.

Pope Francis underlines the need for witness in today's world. He sees movements as called to living consistently the encounter with Jesus that the charism of each movement brings. But it is also a call to "go forth." As he put it during a large gathering at the Vigil of Pentecost on May 18, 2013:

> "Please do not withdraw into yourselves! This is a danger: we shut ourselves up in the parish, with our friends, within the movement, with the like-minded... but do you know what happens? When the Church becomes closed, she becomes an ailing Church, she falls ill! ....The Church must step outside herself. To go where? To the outskirts of existence, whatever they may be, but she must step out. Jesus tells us: 'Go into all the world! Go! Preach! Bear witness to the Gospel!'" (cf. Mk 16:15)

Part 2

Reading the Phenomenon

This section provides keys to reading the phenomenon of ecclesial movements. Although previous chapters have touched on some of this material, it is worthwhile presenting more directly a number of the avenues that theological reflection has pursued regarding movements.

To begin, considering how the movements serve to transmit the Second Vatican Council will lead secondly to an exploration of movements in terms of the polarity between institution and charism suggested by the council's rediscovery of the charismatic principle. Next is the exploration of a perspective that Cardinal Ratzinger advanced in 1998, that movements express apostolic succession in the transmission of the Christ event. Fourth, is a review of the relationship between movements and evangelization. Finally, by way of synthesis, movements are examined in the light of the Church's Marian principle.

Although the keys proposed here are separated for the purposes of exposition and exploration, they all are inter-related. These mutually related viewpoints provide different angles from which to look at the topic of movements.

7

Reception of the Second Vatican Council

The Second Vatican Council concluded in 1965, but the reception of that Pentecostal event is far from complete. In broad terms, reception means the lively, ongoing, Spirit-led process of the Church's "taking over" or appropriating as a whole the vision and implications in doctrine and practice of the council. The reception of Vatican II has been the subject of frequent discussion in recent years.

Various authors have affirmed that the movements seem to have been created precisely so that people can understand and experience the ecclesiology of Vatican II. Two authors—Piero Coda, president of the Sophia University Institute and president of the Italian Theologians' Association, and Ian Ker of Oxford University—offer useful explanations of the function of the movements in the reception of the Second Vatican Council.

The Ecclesiology of Communion as a Modern Form of "Spiritual Exercises"

The new ecclesial movements and communities have made a significant impact in Italy. Piero Coda has long reflected on their import, pursuing many avenues in doing so. In one of his approaches, he considers the meaning of movements in terms of the reception of the church's self-understanding of its mission in the contemporary world as put forward at the Second Vatican Council in light of the mystery of the triune God and the ecclesiology of missionary communion. In their emergence he discerns the Spirit at work, giving flesh and bone to the motifs of mystery, communion, and mission that permeate the council's vision.

Coda acknowledges that post-conciliar initiatives in local churches throughout the world have led many to encounter the letter and spirit of the council's ecclesiology. He notes that the Council of Trent (1545–1563) was followed by effective programmed implementation of its agenda. The council would not have passed into the life-stream of the sixteenth century Catholic Church and profoundly renewed it without exceptional pastors like St. Charles Borromeo. Alongside such great pastors, Coda notes, other charismatic realities and communities that came to life at that time had a great influence in how the council was received. One such example would be Ignatius Loyola and the Jesuits.

In the same way, in the twenty-first century the whole People of God is being called to a faithful and creative reception of the teachings of Vatican II. Clearly, history will remember many distinguished pastors for their initiatives in this regard. The Spirit is certainly working through a renewed appreciation of charisms distributed among the lay faithful as they live out their baptismal priesthood. Coda notes, however, that there is nothing to stop the Holy Spirit, now, as then, from working in the Church not only through the widespread outpouring of charisms in baptism but also through special charisms in the form of new movements and communities.

The Second Vatican Council's emphasis upon Trinitarian unity contributed to the Church's building up a culture of reciprocity that can mend civilization's tattered fabric of co-existence. Word and sacrament generate, nourish, and guide the Church, which is serviced by ministry and charism. But the resultant communion is not just a sacramental and ontological fact. The community of disciples who constitute the Church are called in Christ to live a Trinitarian dynamic of communion among themselves and towards others in the spirit of the "new" commandment, the law of the people of God (see *LG*, 9). This mystery-communion lived out among disciples is the sign and instrument for humanity of encounter with the Risen Christ. In the light of similar notions, Dietrich Bonhoeffer spoke of the Church as "the Christ who is present," Christ existing as community.

According to Coda, the identity and mission of the gifts of the Spirit that animate the ecclesial movements should be read in this broad context of a new emerging culture of reciprocity. For all their limits, the movements' emergence is somehow a sign of the times, related to a new need that the experience of salvation be presented as a dynamic life of communion that begins to fulfill people already within history. In this sense, the movements give flesh to a missionary dynamic of communion, witness, proclamation and incarnation of the gospel in the pluralistic and multi-faceted context of the contemporary world. They express a "come and see" experience (Jn 1:43–51) relevant to contemporary culture.

What Coda proposes, then, is that movements offer an experience of the *anthropological* dynamic inherent in the ecclesiology of communion. Communion means to be "one in Jesus Christ" (Gal 3:28), in that oneness "as I and the Father are one" (Jn 10:30). By being in communion in Christ Jesus, individuals become fully human in God's plan. Certainly, this is a grace that the Church transmits sacramentally. But "being in communion" is also something that Christians must learn, a journey upon which they need to embark in their everyday lives as they follow Jesus Christ and him crucified. Movements provide opportunities, as it were, for people to train or do exercises in a lifestyle of communion. The movements, then, are like modern communitarian forms of "spiritual exercises" in the dynamic of being-in-Christ.

Unity before Distinction

Ian Ker, a respected Oxford scholar, has spent years researching the life and thought of John Henry Newman, leader within the Church of England of the famous nineteenth century Oxford movement. In Newman's thought, Ker finds a rich vein of insight and intuition that guides his reading of post Vatican II developments and the importance of movements in this context.

Newman pointed out that it took 300 years to digest and metabolize the Council of Trent; likewise the significance of Vatican I was not appreciated fully in its own day. The follow-up to a council requires far more than theologians working out the strength of a particular teaching, like lawyers parsing the acts of parliament.

After Vatican II, however, in Ker's view, the significance of *Lumen Gentium's* first chapter, "The Mystery of the Church" was not noticed. He believes that in the long run this chapter might be the most important text of the council. It provides the basis for a complete understanding of the Church as the People of God, a concept that initially after the council was "widely believed to be about the laity, whereas in actual fact it is about all the baptized, that is, all the members of the Church." It was "of considerable importance for the revitalization of the Church" that *Lumen Gentium* did not begin by emphasizing the Church's hierarchical nature, as was normal prior to Vatican II, but by presenting its sacramental nature. The council did not speak of a division between clergy and laity, something quite different from the clericalized vision common before Vatican II. Instead, it highlighted "that the members of the Church are not first and foremost either clergy or laity but simply Christians who all initially receive the three sacraments of initiation, baptism, confirmation, and Eucharist."

Ker considers the new movements and communities important because they represent an experience of the organic and unified community of the baptized as presented in the New Testament and *Lumen Gentium.*

Vatican II encouraged a new perspective, one that begins from the Church of all the baptized and then distinguishes how some serve the organic communion in particular ways. Ker finds the inclusivity of movements attractive. He notes that they "are not ageist, that is, they include the very elderly as well as children, which again sets them apart from other initiatives in collaborative ministry and committees for the bureaucracy of the institutional church."

In *On Consulting the Lay Faithful in Matters of Doctrine*, Newman — as did other nineteenth century theologians — called attention to the organic communion among all the baptized, independent of any one person's particular status in the Church. He found this organic communion first described in the Church of the fourth century. For this reason Ker believes that Newman would have been particularly pleased to see how the first two chapters of *Lumen Gentium* underline this communion.

Evangelization

Ker observes that although Vatican II produced a decree on missionary activity, *Ad Gentes*, it did not really develop the theme of evangelization. Just nine years after the council, Paul VI issued his call for evangelization, *Evangelii Nuntiandi*. Ker considers the movements to be relevant in advancing this aspect, which was implicit in the council but developed afterwards. Piero Coda also considers the theme of evangelization as central in identifying the role and place of the movements in the Church.

8

Institution – Charism

In its rediscovery of the charismatic principle in the Church, the Second Vatican Council established a parameter for reading and interpreting the place of the new ecclesial movements. In time, these movements came to be viewed as an expression of the Church's charismatic element, embedded in the very heart of its inner dynamic between institution and charism. On this basis, John Paul II spoke of them as an expression of the "co-essential" charismatic dimension of the Church:

> I have often had occasion to stress that there is no conflict or opposition in the Church between the institutional dimension and the charismatic dimension, of which the movements are a significant expression. Both are co-essential to the divine constitution of the Church founded by Jesus, because they both help to make the mystery of Christ and his saving work present in the world. Together they aim at renewing in their own ways the self-awareness of the Church, which in a certain sense can be called a "movement" herself, since she is the realization in time and space of the Father's sending of his Son in the power of the Holy Spirit.

To explore more deeply this understanding of movements as an expression of the co-essential charismatic dimension of the Church, this chapter will trace briefly the history of the Church's own teaching and theological reflection on charisms, revisit the Second Vatican Council's teaching (with the assistance of Luigi Sartori and Albert Vanhoye) and then note some theological points made by two well-known twentieth century theologians, Karl Rahner and Avery Dulles.

Charisms — A Historical Overview

The word "charism" is related to many Greek terms, including charis (grace) and eucharistein (to give thanks). The suffix,

-ma, expresses the result of an action indicated by a verb. Broadly speaking, in the New Testament the word signifies "gracious grace" or "gift," but its specific meaning depends upon the context where it appears. Even though the New Testament recounts a great variety of God's gifts and uses the word charism in some significant texts, Albert Vanhoye points out that "these texts do not offer any clear teaching on what are today referred to as 'charisms.'... It is not possible to demonstrate that the word charisma has technical sense in the New Testament."

In the New Testament, Paul uses the word most frequently. He does so in reference to the gift of redemption and eternal life (Rom 5:15–16; 6:23) and to the gifts given to the people of Israel (Rom 11:29). Among charisms Paul also includes bodily healings (1 Cor 12:30) and the graces of the ministers of evangelization (1 Cor 12:8–10; 29–30; Rom 12:6–8), as well as the graces that establish a person in a way of life in the Church — virginity, marriage, pastoral ministry — conferred by the laying on of hands (1 Cor 7: 7; cf. 1 Tim 4: 14; 2 Tim 1:6).

Significantly, Paul uses the metaphor of the body and its members to show that the variety of gifts is not contrary to unity but necessary to it. It builds up the body of Christ. He lists charisms, placing that of the apostles first, those of the prophets second, and others after them (1 Cor 12:27–30). He notes how the Church in Corinth was abundantly favored with charisms (1 Cor 1:4–7; see 1 Cor 12:4–11). He mentions having heard of charisms in the Church of Rome, or having expected to find them there (Rom 12: 4–8). The letter to the Ephesians also contains a list (Eph 4:11–13). Paul is clear: charisms are given for the common good in Christ's body: "To each is given the manifestation of the Spirit for the common good" (1 Cor 12:7).

In the second century, Irenaeus uses the word "charism" for any gift of divine grace, including the Holy Spirit. In reaction to the exaggerated spiritualism of Montanism and Gnostics who rejected the incarnation, denigrated the flesh, and downplayed Church structures, Irenaeus reflects on the whole dynamic of the economy of salvation, underlining the link between the Holy Spirit and the Church. In that regard, he notes that the charisms of the Spirit are placed in the Church, who is kept ever young by the Spirit.

[The faith transmitted by the Church] by work of the Holy Spirit, like a precious deposit contained in a valuable vase, is ever rejuvenated and also rejuvenates the vase that contains it. To the Church, in fact, was entrusted the gift of God (see Jn 4:10) like a breath that is blown into the living being shaped from the soil of the ground (see Gen 2:7), so that all her members, by participating in it, are vivified by it; and in her has been deposited the communion with Christ, that is the Holy Spirit... In fact, "God has appointed, in the Church first apostles, second prophets, third teachers" (see 1 Cor 12:28) and imbued her with all the remaining operation of the Spirit (see 1 Cor 12:11).... For where the Church is, there too is the Spirit of God; and where the Spirit of God is, there too are the Church and every form of grace.

With the rise of the mendicant religious orders and the need to discern the authenticity of new experiences that were appearing in the Medieval Age (for instance the case of St. Brigid of Sweden's private revelations), a new interest in charisms and their discernment grew up. In its theology, the Medieval Latin commentators and teachers did not use the word "charism," but rather "gratia" or grace. They distinguished between the gifts of the Holy Spirit necessary for salvation, i.e. the gifts that arise from sanctifying grace (*gratiae gratum faciens*, grace making gracious) and other gifts of the Spirit called gratuitous gifts (*gratiae gratis data*, grace freely given and conferred on a person or group for the salvation of others). These latter correspond to what we today call "charisms."

St. Thomas Aquinas (1225–1274) also distinguishes between sanctifying grace and gratuitous gifts (*gratiae gratis datae*). He notes the usefulness of the latter for spreading and confirming the faith. He places his treatment of them right in the heart of his treatise on morality, as if to underline their centrality in the life of the Church. Reflecting on the life of the Spirit in the lives of the faithful and in the Church, Aquinas presents the Holy Spirit as the soul vivifying the body which is the Church, giving efficacy to all ministries and sacraments in the Church. He uses two key words to describe the work of the Spirit in human beings. By "inhabitation," the Spirit dwells within them and by "innovation" makes them new. On this basis, in the 1980s Francis Sullivan concluded that "there is no reason why Catholics, who believe that they have already received the Holy Spirit in their sacramental initiation, should not look forward to a new 'sending' of the Spirit to them, which would move them from the 'state of grace' in which they already are into some 'new act' or 'new state of grace.'"

After the Middle Ages, theological reflection on the topic of charisms was limited, in no small part because theology and spirituality had a certain parting of the ways. Increasingly, charismatic experiences such as those associated with the rise of the mendicant orders and those manifest in later founders such as Teresa of Avila and Ignatius of Loyola came to be viewed from a hagiographical and spiritual perspective.

In the nineteenth century, however, the German legal theorist R. Sohm (1841–1917) explored anew the notion of "charism."

In reaction to Sohm's thesis, the German theologian and church historian, Adolf von Harnack (1851–1930), contended that the early Church contained two types of ministry—the universal charismatic and the local administrative. He gave priority to the charismatic.

At the same time in history, the language of charism was beginning to re-appear in Church documents. The First Vatican Council (1869–1870) mentions "charism" in an apologetic sense, linking it to the role of the hierarchy and the Roman pontiff's prerogative of infallibility. The reference in Vatican I was Christological: in instituting the Church, Jesus Christ promised to assist Peter and gave him the grace to do so.

Pius XII referred to charism in the encyclical *Mystici Corporis* (1943) and again at the canonization of Pius X. On the one hand, he presents charism in terms of a miraculous gift that relates to the extraordinary phenomena associated with saints and mystics. On the other hand, however, he also broadens the notion of charism, underlining gifts given for the Church as a whole. In other words, charisms have an ecclesial role. Viewing the Church as an organic body, he speaks of charism as an element, indeed almost a principle of the structure of the Church and affirms: "One must not think, however, that this ordered or 'organic' structure of the body of the Church contains only hierarchical elements and with them is complete; or, as an opposite opinion holds, that it is composed only of those who enjoy charismatic gifts —though members gifted with miraculous powers will never be lacking in the Church." Pius XII seems to believe that charisms can be found also on the more general level of ecclesial life. Jesus Christ, he affirms, foresaw and ordered both the charismatic and institutional aspects, both equally informed by the Holy Spirit.

Pius XII clearly recognizes the creator Spirit always at work in the Church—not just in the early Church—and believes in the free action of the Spirit throughout its history, distributing gifts also outside the hierarchy.

Vatican II

The documents of the Second Vatican Council make fifteen direct references to the notion of charism, not including the many other cognate terms or notions such as "gift," "graces," "operations," "virtues," "ministry," "vocation," "munera" (office). Accordingly, the Italian theologian Luigi Sartori contends that in the Council's documents a wealth of texts, around a hundred, could be said to refer to the theme of charisms.

Nevertheless, Vatican II teaches clearly that, as Rino Fisichella puts it, "the prophets and the prophetic charism can't be relegated hastily only to the period of the primitive Church; they are always a constituent part of the Church and always possess a permanent and irreplaceable significance for the Church."

Charisms within a Trinitarian Ecclesiology

As already noted, the Second Vatican Council presents a Christo-centric and Trinitarian vision of the Church. Created to mirror Christ who leads the faithful in the Spirit to the bosom of the Father, the Church is the realm of mutual being-for-one-another in a way that resembles the life of the Trinity. The Spirit is the principle of the Church's dynamic unity. The third divine person maintains the Church as a movement of eternal youthfulness awaiting the coming Christ: "The Spirit and the Bride say to the Lord Jesus: Come!" (Rev 22:17; LG 4).

Charisms, given by the Spirit, play an important role in this eschatological tension in the Church guided by the Spirit towards its fulfillment at the end of time. They allow for the distinctiveness of diverse ways of building up the one body of Christ as it strives towards its fulfillment when God will be "all in all." The unity of the Church, in other words, is understood eschatologically as the recapitulation, gathering and appreciation of the multiform grace of God as it moves towards the full and perfect life that is full participation in the triune life of God.

The Council encourages attentiveness to the "most simple and common" charisms. In so doing it underscores the variety of gifts as distinct aspects linked to the freedom of each baptized person.

Charism and Hierarchy

The Council affirms that different charisms should be welcomed "with gratitude and consolation" but also states that "judgment as to their genuineness and proper use belongs to those who are appointed leaders in the Church, to whose special competence it belongs, not in-deed to extinguish the Spirit, but to test all things and hold fast to that which is good (see 1 Thes 5:12 and 19–21)." Interestingly, Sartori remarks that the Second Vatican Council was held in an atmosphere of optimistic recovery of trust in charisms. It wasn't particularly concerned about the issue of the criteria of discernment. It is simply stated in a generic sense that the judgment regarding the genuineness of charisms is up to the hierarchy. St. Paul's warning about the discernment of spirits is referred to but without giving precise norms.

The Primacy of Love

Echoing Paul, the Council also points to a central theme that underlies any consideration of the relationship of charism and institution — charity. Love, in fact, is the prime principle of the whole life of the Church. It is at the heart of the sacramentality of the Church. A charism is authentic not only if it expresses charity but also if it contributes to making the general charism of the Church emerge, that is, its nature as the gift of love offered by Christ to humanity. Ultimately, true charisms serve to love, to build up the Church so that it may be for the world a sign and instrument of unity and salvation in Christ.

Love becomes an art to be lived both by those entrusted with the task of investigating and judging the authenticity of charisms as well as by those endowed with new charisms to be communicated to the whole Church. With regard to those whose task it is to discern the authenticity of charisms, Alois Grillmeier acknowledges this task is "one of the most difficult arts in the guidance of men and Churches, and though final judgment rests with the holders of office, this does not dispense or exclude the faithful as a whole from being involved in the duty of investigation." With regard to founders or communities and by extension, members of movements, Castellano Cervera describes what is required as a great love for the Church, "the passion to serve (the Church), the true sense of the Church, the 'feeling with the Church' and the feeling Church (*sentire Ecclesiam*)."

In consoling fashion, when the Council declares that "the Spirit instructs and directs the Church with different hierarchical and charismatic gifts," it is also issuing a reminder that hierarchical gifts are also gifts of the Spirit. Through the action of the Spirit pastors are made "fit and ready to assume" their ecclesial responsibilities in a personal, spiritual fashion. This is a point Benedict XVI often underlined. Bishops, priests and deacons receive charism through sacramental ordination.

Ultimately, any reflection on the interaction of charism and institution in terms of love needs to draw on the model of all love—the triune God. The German theologian and bishop Klaus Hemmerle, writing expressly in reference to the new ecclesial movements, suggests exercising the dynamic of *perichoresis* (a lively, ever new, mutual dwelling in one another) in the mutual relationships of institutional office holders and charismatics in the Church.

Karl Rahner

The theological writings of Karl Rahner (1904–1984) were important in the reception of the Council's doctrine on charisms. Charisms may be extraordinary but they also become daily bread, normal and usual in the life of the Church. Though not referring directly to new ecclesial movements as such, Rahner's theology and commentary on charisms is important in interpreting their significance.

Avery Dulles

The late Avery Cardinal Dulles has been acclaimed as "perhaps the most productive and respected American Catholic theologian of our time." Robert Imbelli comments that "in Dulles, the oft-lauded Catholic 'both/and' approach found an exemplary practitioner. He was steadfast in his fidelity to *Lumen Gentium's* insistence that the church of Christ consists of two inseparable dimensions: the charismatic and the institutional. To speak of the 'institutional church' as though there were some other, purely spiritual church preserved in Platonic perfection would be fantasy."

His 1992 book *The Craft of Theology: From Symbol to System* offers a summary of his ecclesial vision. Though his book, *Models of the Church,* contains surprisingly few references to charisms, Dulles dedicates an important chapter of *A Church to Believe in: Discipleship and the Dynamics of Freedom* to this theme.

The Church never has been, and never can be, without institutional elements. The Church never has been, and never can be, without charismatic elements. A Church without charisms could only be a Church without grace. Charisms and institutions seem to have grown concurrently, most strikingly in the period after Pentecost. The charismatic lives off the institutional. The institutional in the Church lives off the charismatic.

Conclusion

This chapter has explored the significance of charisms, particularly how charism and institution are co-essential in the life of the Church. John Paul II and others have presented the dynamic between charism and institution as a way of putting in proper context the phenomenon of movements in the Church today. The last word, perhaps, belongs to one of the great bearers of a charism in the history of the Church—Francis of Assisi. Like other founders of great movements of reform such as Benedict, Ignatius of Loyola, and Teresa of Avila, Francis was a devoted servant of the Church in its institutional or hierarchical-sacramental dimension. Immersed in the heritage of the Church they were able to love, transform and renew it. In his testament of 1226, the year of his death, Francis writes:

> Afterwards the Lord gave me, and gives me still, such faith in priests who live according to the rite of the holy Roman Church because of their order that, were they to persecute me, I would still want to have recourse to them. And if I had as much wisdom as Solomon and found impoverished priests of this world, I would not preach in the parishes against their will. I desire to respect, love, and honor them and all others as my lords. And I do not want to consider any sin in them because I discern the Son of God in them and they are my lords. And I act in this way because, in this world, I see nothing corporally of the Most High Son of God except His most holy Body and Blood which they receive and they alone administer to others.

9

Movements and Apostolic Succession

In his May 1998 address to the World Congress of Ecclesial Movements, Cardinal Joseph Ratzinger suggested that movements be considered an expression of apostolic succession. In many ways this talk remains the "Magna Carta" for a theological and ecclesiological reading of the movements. This chapter offers an exposition of Ratzinger's main points, recognizing that that theme of apostolic succession is much discussed, particularly in the fields of ecumenism and Church ministry.

Unsatisfactory Dialectic Approaches

In the first part of his talk Cardinal Ratzinger acknowledges both the value of and the limitations of different interpretative keys. For instance, although the institution-charism duality might seem the most useful model for thinking through the theological place of movements, it risks setting up a dialectic between institution and charism; such an "antithesis between the two terms gives no satisfactory description of the reality of the Church." Although the Church indeed does contain institutions of primarily human and sociological origin that carry out various roles of administration, organization and co-ordination, its fundamental institutional structure is linked with the sacramental ministry, which is itself a gift of the Spirit. The dialectic breaks down because the service of bishops, priests and deacons itself is charismatic, that is, a gift of the Spirit.

The Church comes into existence first and foremost by God's call, in other words, at the charismatic and pneumatological level through the sacraments. Because the Church comes into being through divine means, it cannot be interpreted through institutional or sociological criteria alone. Indeed, Ratzinger notes that if we attempt to distinguish between institution and charism, the concept of institution "falls to bits in our hands as soon as we try to give it a precise theological connotation." Institution is charism!

Ratzinger concludes, moreover, that in order to prevent institutional hardening, sacramental ministry must be charismatically understood and lived. The Church "must not over-institutionalize herself."

He then examines the dialectic between the Christological and pneumatological view of the Church in contemporary theology. Some maintain that sacraments belong to the Christological-incarnational aspect of the Church, supplemented by its pneumatological-charismatic dimension. Here again, however, Ratzinger sees a limit. Understood dialectically, such a distinction again seems to fall to pieces. A distinction does need to be drawn between Christ and the Spirit; nevertheless, "Just as the three persons of the Trinity should be treated not as a communion of three gods, but as the one triune God, so the distinction between Christ and Spirit can be rightly understood only when their diversity helps us better to understand their unity." The Spirit cannot be rightly understood without Christ and Christ cannot be rightly understood without the Spirit. Moreover, examining the inter-relationship between the Spirit and the Risen-crucified Christ as reflected in the Tradition, Ratzinger arrives at the need to reflect on the theme of apostolic succession. He returns to this relationship as a main concept in answering his initial question of how best to understand movements in the Church.

A third model that might interpret and explain the relationship between the sacramental-institutional side of the Church and the ever-new irruptions of the Spirit is hierarchy and prophecy. As Ratzinger puts it, "Building on Luther's interpretation of Scripture in terms of the dialectic of Law and Gospel, there are those who place particular stress on the dialectic between the cultic-sacerdotal aspect on the one hand and the prophetic aspect of salvation history on the other." From such a perspective, movements would be an expression of the prophetic aspect. This interpretation, he feels, has value but "It is extremely imprecise and hence unusable in this form." Again, Ratzinger seems concerned about the dialectic of hierarchy and prophecy. While not going into detail, he remarks there is no Scriptural justification for a dualism between a prophetic class and hierarchical order. Biblical prophets actually defended the Law by vindicating its true meaning. In the Old Covenant, they were never viewed as a class in contrast with a class of priests (see Amos 7:10–17; 1 Kings 22; Jer 37:19). Again, Ratzinger comments that the various functions within the Church should not be viewed dialectically, but organically: "What only remains true is that ... God continually inspires prophetic men and women ... who would not derive the necessary strength in the normal course of the 'institution' to make ... charismatic appeal to the Church."

Opting for a Historical Approach

Cardinal Ratzinger concludes that using a dialectic of principles is unsatisfactory in trying to determine the place of ecclesial movements in the Church. He chooses instead an historical approach. He examines the history of the Church, highlighting the link between apostolic succession and apostolic movements. In doing so he makes significant theological clarifications.

Ratzinger explains that apostolic succession does not mean that the faithful become independent of the Spirit through the continuous chain of succession from one generation to the next. The link between the "once" and the "for always" of the Christ event is made visible in the sacraments. The sacraments transmit the presence in pneumatical form of the Church's historical origin in every age. In other words, the Lord himself, in the power of the Spirit, works through the sacraments to build up his Church. The originating event of Jesus Christ is communicated by the gift of the Holy Spirit who is the Spirit of the Risen Lord: "The Incarnation does not stop with the historical Jesus.... The 'historical Jesus' has eternal significance precisely because his 'flesh' is transformed in the resurrection, so that he can make himself present in all places and at all times in the power of the Holy Spirit."

The early Church on the one hand included the itinerant apostolic ministry and on the other the services of the local church, which gradually took on the fixed form of bishop, priest and deacon. When these universal itinerant missionaries died out, the bishops who presided over the local churches that had been set up by the apostles came to recognize, as the second century bishop and theologian Irenaeus of Lyons states, that they are now the successors of the apostles and the apostolic mission lay on their shoulders. Apostolic succession entailed guaranteeing a sacramental continuity and unity of the faith. It entailed ensuring the continuation of Jesus' mission to make all nations disciples and bring the gospel to the ends of the earth.

Apostolic Movements in the History of the Church

Ratzinger notes that in the second century, as the supra-local universal ministry was dying out and being absorbed by the local episcopal ministry (not without the risks of stagnation), a new phenomenon emerged — the monastic movement. Following the person often considered the founder of monasticism, Abbot Anthony (c.251–356) into the desert, the first monks moved beyond the local in "a deliberate abandonment of the firmly established structure of the local Church." Fleeing a Christianity that was progressively adapting itself to the needs of secular life, Anthony's choice actually "gave rise to a new spiritual fatherhood; and this spiritual fatherhood, while it had no directly missionary character, did nonetheless supplement the fatherhood of bishops and priests by the power of a whole pneumatic life." Indeed, "the monastic movement created a new centre of life that did not abolish the local ecclesial structure of the post-apostolic Church, but that did not simply coincide with it either." Monasticism was "active ... as a life-giving force, a kind of reservoir from which the local Church could draw truly spiritual clergy in whom the fusion of institution and charism was constantly renewed."

The fourth century founder of communal monasticism, Basil (330–379), recognized that the movement to follow Jesus Christ in an uncompromising fashion could not be merged completely with the local Church. In the second draft of a rule, Basil describes the monastic movement as a "transitional form between a group of committed Christians open to the Church as a whole and a self-organizing and self-institutionalizing monastic order." The monastic community was to serve as leaven, a "small group for the revitalization of the whole."

Noting that the emergence of this new dimension of ecclesial life did not coincide with the configuration of the local churches, Ratzinger presents a brief historical overview of the apostolic movements of the Church's journey in fidelity to its apostolic origins and form.

The monasteries, which began as points of spiritual renewal, soon developed into a great missionary movement. In the tenth century, a reform movement started within the Benedictine order.

Thirteenth century mendicant orders such as the Franciscans and Dominicans wanted to recall the Church to the whole message of the gospel and proclaim it beyond the frontiers of Christendom to the ends of the earth.

The evangelization movements of the sixteenth century embarked on a world-wide mission in America, Africa and Asia. Cardinal Ratzinger mentions the Jesuits who were prominent among these evangelizers, as well as the Dominicans and Franciscans who "thanks to their enduring missionary impulse, did not lag far behind."

The evangelizing dynamic continued in the spate of movements that began in the nineteenth century. Surveying the whole history of the Church, Ratzinger acknowledges the co-responsibility of women in the apostolic life and in its universal mission, particularly in the nineteenth century.

Drawing his review of apostolic movements in the history of the Church to a close, Ratzinger concludes that the papacy did not create these movements; rather, the popes saw their missionary potential and became their main supporters. This could happen precisely because the Pope is not merely the bishop of the local Church of Rome. His unique universal ministry leads him to have a special interest in encouraging movements whose apostolic dynamism goes beyond the structure and range of the local Church.

Ratzinger summarizes his review by underlining how, on the one hand, the local Church "necessarily determined by the episcopal ministry is the supporting structure that permanently upholds the edifice of the Church throughout the ages," binding it to the Paschal events of Jesus' life, death and resurrection. On the other hand, the history of the Church also has been "traversed by successive waves of movements that renew the universalistic aspect of her apostolic mission and thus serve to foster the spiritual vitality and truth of the local Churches."

Movements and the Notion of Apostolic Succession

Based on his survey of the main apostolic movements in the history of the Church, Cardinal Ratzinger concludes that the concept of apostolic succession must be broadened and deepened. Certainly, the sacramental structure of the Church forms the core of the notion of apostolic succession: "The sacrament means that the Church lives and is continually recreated by the Lord as 'creature of the Holy Spirit.'" The Church, bound to the unique and unrepeatable Incarnation and the Easter events, has a Christological-incarnational aspect. Simultaneously, it also has a Christological-pneumatological side, that is, "the making present of this event in the power of the Holy Spirit" in each new era of history, which "guarantees at once the newness and the continuity of the living Church."

Conclusion

Because movements are part of the apostolic dimension of the Church, those involved in them need to recognize more clearly how they are called to follow Christ radically. Cardinal Ratzinger comments that "the wish to lead the apostolic life must be fundamental for them in every period." This apostolic life creates freedom for service, particularly proclamation of the gospel as the missionary element par excellence, with charity as its inner source.

10

Movements and Evangelization

The 2008 Synod on the Word of God in the life and mission of the Church "recognized with gratitude that the ecclesial movements and the new communities are a great force for evangelization in our times and an incentive to the development of new ways of proclaiming the Gospel." Evangelization, which is said to be the very identity of the Church, is seriously challenged both by the new geographical distribution of Catholics and by the drama, especially in the Western world, of the split between faith and culture. Movements have often been interpreted in terms of a providential response to these contemporary challenges. Considering this key for interpreting the significance of movements demands a working definition of evangelization. It has been pointed out that there are at least seventy-nine definitions of what authors mean by evangelism or evangelization! Pope Paul VI's words, therefore, provide a valuable synthesis:

> Evangelization ... is a complex process made up of varied elements: the renewal of humanity, witness, explicit proclamation, inner adherence, entry into the community, acceptance of signs, apostolic initiative. These elements ... are complementary and mutually enriching. Each one must always be seen in relationship with the others.

Since the early twentieth century, there has been an enormous shift in mission and evangelization. As Vatican II put it, "The human race is involved in a new stage of history. Profound and rapid changes are spreading by degrees around the whole world." In *Transforming Mission: Paradigm Shifts in Theology of Mission*, David Bosch contends that the 1910 Edinburgh missionary conference marked the "all-time high-water mark in Western missionary enthusiasm, the zenith of the optimistic and pragmatist approach to missions." Western Christians saw themselves with a vast mission of renewing the face of the earth, given they had the possibilities to do so. Works and initiatives abounded — mission stations, schools, hospitals and shelters for the poor. John R. Mott, the long-serving leader of the YMCA and the World Student Christian Federation, was convinced that given the rate of the progress of modern science and the opportunities it was offering, the world could be evangelized in his generation, opening door after door to the power of the gospel. Providence and revelation were combining in such a remarkable manner that, *"the victory may not be easy, but it is sure."*

Europe and America saw themselves at the center of Christianity, with "missions" at the world's periphery. In 1900, 85% of Christians lived in Europe and America. Of the 1200 delegates at the Edinburgh conference in 1910, 1170 were Western (500 British, 500 American and 170 from the rest of Europe). Only 30 delegates attended from India, China and Japan, and none from either Africa or Latin America.

By 2000, however, the percentage of the world's Christians in Europe had fallen to under 40% and by 2050 it could possibly be under 30%. In 1960 over 50% of Catholics lived in North America and Europe; by 2000 that had fallen to 38%. In 2010, over 50% of the world's Catholics lived in South America.

However beyond mere statistics, a deeper reality is operating. Since the early twentieth century, practical atheism has spread throughout the Western world, driving a wedge between the Transcendent and day-to-day cultural expressions of life such as economics, politics, family life and education. These vast issues defy easy categorization. There is something of an irony, then, that in the very year (2010) marking the hundredth anniversary of the Edinburgh Conference, whose Western-centered perspective surveyed the rest of the world in an optimistic drive to bring the gospel everywhere, Benedict XVI established a new Pontifical Council "whose principal task will be to promote a renewed evangelization in the countries where the first proclamation of the faith has already resonated and where Churches with an ancient foundation exist but are experiencing the progressive secularization of society and a sort of 'eclipse of the sense of God,' which pose a challenge to finding appropriate means to propose anew the perennial truth of Christ's Gospel."

Compared to 1910 and its sense of mission, the Christian world is in a very different place. In many ways the mission Christ entrusted to the Church "is still very far from completion"; indeed, "this mission is still only beginning." The West needs a new "leap of faith," both in terms of the act of faith and in the way of expressing and communicating it. At the same time a vast worldwide network of evangelical and charismatic movements has emerged rapidly, especially in the Southern hemisphere, calling for the Catholic Church to find new ways to ensure its members have valid, attractive community experiences.

What a 1963 missionary conference said still rings true — mission today is to be carried out on *"six continents ... from everywhere to everywhere."* The Second Vatican Council marked a major turning point in the Catholic Church.

In creating the Council for a New Evangelization, Benedict XVI has taken up a theme, the New Evangelization, that John Paul II had made the central motif of his pontificate.

Mystery, Communion and Mission

As the Church looks out for such "new ways," it must attend to what the Spirit indicated at the great Pentecostal event of the Second Vatican Council. At a 2000 Congress on Catechesis and Evangelization, Cardinal Joseph Ratzinger offered his personal recollection of preparations for the Council. As a young theologian, he had accompanied Cardinal Frings as an adviser. Like many others, in their preparatory deliberations, the German bishops were beginning to focus on the topic of Church as the issue for the Council. Ratzinger recalls Frings telling him, however, that at a certain point during their discussions, the elderly but much-esteemed Bishop Buchberger of the diocese of Regensburg offered his simple advice: "My brothers, at the Council you must above all talk about God. This is what is most important." Ratzinger agreed that "the Second Vatican Council certainly did intend to subordinate what it said about the Church to what it said about God."

Although the Council sought to reflect on the Church, its clarion call became Jesus Christ and the life of Triune God. That life opens up for human beings through encounter with Christ in

the world, where the Holy Spirit "in a manner known only to God
offers to everyone the possibility of being associated with this
paschal mystery." The Church, icon of the Trinity, evangelizes
through its unity, which mirrors and participates in the triune
unity of God. The ecclesial movements contribute to evangelization in three ways that correspond to the three central motifs of
Vatican II—mystery, communion and mission.

The charism at work in an ecclesial movement or community
instills in those who are part of it profound conviction and promotes missionary drive. This drive is based on a personal and
vibrant encounter with Jesus Christ that transforms individuals'
lives, leading them to take as their own Paul's words, "Woe betide
me if I do not proclaim the gospel!" (1 Cor 9:16). Such persons
want to witness to a new life, a life of communion rooted in the
God who has revealed himself eschatologically in Jesus Christ.
This return to an original experience of the gospel of the crucified and risen Christ becomes urgent in view of the challenge of
post-modernity and globalization. In a 1995 essay Avery Dulles
commented that "too many Catholics of our day seem never
to have met the Lord. They know a certain amount about him
from the teaching of the Church, but they lack direct, personal
familiarity." Only a personal experience of the faith can insert
the leaven of the Kingdom of God into the human and cultural
contexts where the future of the millennium will be determined.
Proclaiming principles is important, but not enough. That's why
the evangelizers need to be evangelized. And for that something
more is needed. Benedict XVI explains:

> In fact, when, in the view of many people, the Catholic faith
> is no longer the common patrimony of society and, often,
> seen as threatened and obscured by the "gods" and masters
> of this world, only with great difficulty can the faith touch
> the hearts of people by means simple speeches or moral ap-
> peals, and even less by a general appeal to Christian values.
> The courageous and integral appeal to principles is essential
> and indispensable; yet simply proclaiming the message does
> not penetrate to the depths of people's hearts, it does not
> touch their freedom, it does not change their lives. What
> attracts is, above all, the encounter with believing persons

who, through their faith, draw others to the grace of Christ by bearing witness to him.

At a time when personal, communitarian, and social witness is central in evangelization, movements provide experiences of a life of communion that others can "come and see" (see Jn 1:46). At a time when the Church senses the need to "launch into the deep," movements also provide new forms and strategies of witness, dialogue, and proclamation as well as incarnation of the gospel and service of the poor. This is important because evangelization does not come about only through the parish. People spend much of their day in a range of different environments from family to sport, from work to entertainment, from travel to the internet, and with a range of people, both religious and non-religious. As Bishop Porteous comments, "To attempt to catalogue the ways in which this work of evangelization is being realized is impossible. They are legion."

Taking into account the importance of missionary communion, the German Jesuit theologian Medhard Kehl writes that the new movements "represent an authentically Christian response to the challenge of the contemporary cultural situation in proportion as they try expressly to live ecclesial 'communio' in conditions of modern individualization."

Movements and People's Spiritual Needs

In many ways, people today search for an experience of salvation not simply as a distant future reality but as an experience of human fulfillment and realization within history, here and now. At a major conference in Rome during the Jubilee Year 2000, Cardinal Ratzinger spoke in clear terms of the urgent need for such a new evangelization. Describing its heart as demonstrating a path towards happiness and teaching an art of living that many want to learn, he pointed out that the classic means of spreading the gospel such as Mass, the sacraments, preaching, even institutional commitment to the causes of justice and peace are essential, but not sufficient. Something more is needed, a new way.

A Gospel "Leaven" in Society

Some who critique movements and their significance for the Church's evangelizing mission sense in them a certain naiveté, or the risk of falling into a regressive and traditional Catholicism. Sometimes movements are seen as emphasizing private interior experience or as promoting a triumphalistic "new Christendom" that contradicts the deepest intentions of Vatican II.

The Council did propose a new vision of the Catholic Church as a presence in the world of culture and society to supplant the notion of *Christendom*, a term that suggests a combined religious and civil power that the Church has left behind. Nor does the Church want to present itself as a "perfect society" (*societas perfecta*), an alternative, self-sufficient order that parallels or stands in opposition to cultures that organize themselves according to non-Christian principles. In rejecting the desire for privilege or hegemony, at Vatican II the Church took up instead the difficult and risky logic of seeing itself as a gospel "leaven" in an increasingly pluralistic society searching for common points of convergence.

In their finest expression, movements have emerged to respond to just such needs. They have been born from the impulse to maintain the original baptismal source experience as a living historical presence of Christianity in the world. They want to serve the Church, which sees itself as casting the seed of the Word of God widely in culture; not closing in on itself in self-defense, but voyaging into the deep with courage and prudence (always in communion with the bishops), sowing the Word of God in the vast field of history.

The movements can be a true leaven in society by promoting a full humanism that finds its measure in the person of Jesus Christ. The life of communion and co-responsibility that movements live can permeate civil society, providing a creative and critical resource for the participative praxis of democracy. And that too can be evangelization.

11

The Ecclesial Movements
and the Marian Principle

During preparations for the Great Jubilee of 2000, John Paul II commented, "At the dawn of the new millennium, we notice with joy the emergence of the 'Marian profile' of the Church that summarizes the deepest concerns of the conciliar renewal." The new ecclesial movements were among the signs he referred to as that profile's manifestation. This "Marian profile" is a fifth key to reading the phenomenon of movements in our time.

This line of reflection includes several strands. First, many movements draw inspiration from Mary, the first disciple of Jesus. Sometimes stories of their origins are even linked to Marian feast days or shrines. For instance, the Schoenstatt movement began on October 18, 1914, when Joseph Kentenich (1885–1968) and a few others sealed their "covenant of love" with Mary. The Teams of Our Lady movement began at the end of the 1930s when a number of married couples, under the guidance of Fr. Henri Caffarel, began to meet every month in each other's houses. The Emmanuel Community is named after the passage of Scripture, "Behold, a young woman shall conceive and bear a son, and shall call his name Emmanuel" (Is 7:14; see Mt 1:23).

Many movements, to a greater or lesser degree, draw inspiration in their story or spirituality from some aspect of Mary's life or doctrine about her. As mentioned in earlier chapters, the Legion of Mary movement drew its inspiration from Louis de Montfort. The Focolare Movement is also officially known as the "Work of Mary." Many Charismatic Renewal communities highlight Mary as their model.

Von Balthasar

Swiss theologian Hans Urs von Balthasar, a man keenly sensitive to what has flowered in the Church's garden, reflected on this Marian principle and its connection to the movements. These sources of renewal and hope have come about, he explains, not from the hierarchy of the Church or out of necessity or utility. Rather, they express what he calls the subjective, Marian principle of the Church. His encouraging and clarifying reflection on this phenomenon is important. For instance Libero Gerosa, a canonist, claims that theologians and the magisterium itself owe much to von Balthasar, especially his complex and organic thought about the two poles of ecclesiology, the two central dimensions – the Marian and the Petrine—around which all discussion of the Church revolves.

In particular, von Balthasar reflects on two co-essential principles that form the epicenter of the Church as a dynamic sphere of mutual love: the Petrine point of unity (the Pope but also the hierarchical-sacramental structure of the Church, in terms of the hierarchy's role in community building through apostolic preaching and sacraments); and the Marian point of unity in terms of a living actualization of the gospel in holiness, witness and transformation of the world. In an address to the Roman Curia, taking up von Balthasar's line of thought, John Paul II spoke of the Marian profile as equally fundamental and characteristic of the Church to the Petrine, if not more so. Benedict XVI has also elaborated upon this theme.

Mary and the Spirit

By concluding its constitution on the Church, *Lumen Gentium*, with a chapter on Mary, the Second Vatican Council directed attention to the woman who is an "integral part of the economy of the communication of the Trinity to the human race." Mary stands at the place where the drama of divine freedom and human freedom—and history—intersect in Jesus Christ. She represents a co-operating response (see 1 Cor 3:9) to grace, to the divine invitation to enter the rhythm of "trinitization" of humankind: "... That they may all be one. As you, Father, are in me and I am in you, may they also be in us, so that the world may believe that you have sent me.... I in them and you in me, that they may become completely one, so that the world may know that you have sent me and have loved them even as you have loved me" (Jn 17:21–23).

More and more, Mary's link with the Holy Spirit has been explored. This first disciple of Jesus worked together with the Holy Spirit to allow the event of Jesus' life, death and resurrection to take place in history. The gospels present Mary on three occasions in particular: the "yes" of the Annunciation (Lk 1:38), the second "yes" at the foot of the Cross (Jn 19:25–27) and her presence in the midst of the community awaiting Pentecost (Acts 1:14). In Luke's Gospel, when Mary says: "Behold I am the servant of the Lord, let what you have said be done unto me" (1:38), she lets the Word become flesh in her. It becomes history through her. Representative of humanity, she lets the Word live her. That first "yes" in a sense contains all future "yeses." It's a "yes" every person can repeat. It's the total readiness to let God's action become history through us, with us and in us.

Saying "yes" to God is never simply a private or individual matter. The iconic moment presented in the Fourth Gospel, that of Mary at the foot of the Cross, reveals that. For himself, Jesus substitutes the beloved disciple (see Jn 19:25–27). Mary "loses," as it were, "her" God and, in the place of Jesus, welcomes one of his disciples. In doing so she opens without reserve to others, to every person, to the whole of humanity, building up the new "Christified" transformed humanity. She and the beloved disciple form the first cell of mutual love at the heart of the Church.

Objective-Subjective Holiness

Von Balthasar reflects on Mary's link with the Spirit in terms of objective and subjective holiness. The Spirit, he says, gifts the Church with both forms of holiness. Objectively, from the very beginnings of the Church, in the power of the Holy Spirit, the Crucified-Risen Christ works through the Word of God proclaimed, the sacraments administered and ministerial guidance. These three foundations of ecclesial life — Word, sacraments and ministry — constitute the sure objective basis of the Church as a people gathered in communion and called to communicate the life of communion. As such these pillars form the "rock" that upholds the whole edifice. In this sense, through his personalist ecclesiology von Balthasar links them with the "Petrine" (from Peter, rock) principle. Ultimately, this "rock" is Christ himself present in the midst of the community, the Risen Crucified Christ who speaks and works in the Word, the sacraments, and his ministers.

Mary, who von Balthasar calls "the supreme, normative subjectivity" of the Church, is the particular model and interior form of the receiving and actualizing, the making history of the life in the Church that comes through objective sacramental-hierarchical means.

The history of the Church is the time between the Christ event and humankind's letting it happen, their response, one that will be complete only when all the Church and humanity become totally open to God and his gifts, inhabited by the Word, gathered in Christ and so permeated by the Spirit of the Risen Christ, Christified and Trinitized. The Church's pilgrim journey revolves around the inter-action of the objective-institutional and subjective-charismatic polarities of holiness that shape its members being in Christ.

Charisms and Movements

According to von Balthasar, within this objective-subjective polarity of the Church's holiness the charisms of founders of orders, communities, and movements work in synergy with the apostolic ministry. In doing so, they reflect the Marian dimension of the Church. On the journey towards the fullness of truth, the Holy Spirit underlines, highlights, and renders operative a particular aspect of the infinite mystery of Christ that responds to a particular need or feature of an era. Each of the charisms, von Balthasar affirms, is like a bolt of lightning, destined to illuminate a new or original point of God's will for the Church in a given era. Each charism shows a new way to follow Christ, a new illustration of how to live the gospel, a new interpretation of revelation. The movements that charisms generate are expressions of the life of communion, communicated sacramentally, taking on ever new forms along the Church's journey.

Accordingly, the presence of new movements that have come to life through charisms—involving all the vocations of the Church—is a sign of the emergence of the Church's Marian profile, a profile that needs to be rediscovered. Along this way, the movements' focus on spirituality, their mainly lay profile, their strong ecclesial sense and evangelizing dynamism provide a stimulus for the Church to recognize its full identity.

Von Balthasar's own invitation to understand the nature of the Church in its deepest profile by looking to Mary provides a fitting conclusion to this chapter:

> Perhaps it is precisely our time that especially needs to see Mary. To see her as she shows herself, not as we would like to imagine her. To see her, if at all, in order not to forget her essential role in the work of salvation and in the Church. In reality, she shows herself and defines herself as the archetypal Church, whose form we have to take as our pattern. That means every single Christ, and yet it may mean even more: our image of what Church is. We are busily refashioning and improving this Church according to the needs of the times, the criticisms of our opponents, and our own models. But do we not lose sight in all this of the only perfect criterion, that is, of the archetype? Should we not keep our eyes fixed on Mary in all of our reforms—not in order to multiply Marian feasts, devotions, or even definitions in the Church, but simply in order to remain aware of what Church, ecclesial spirit, ecclesial conduct really are?

Appendix

Listing of Movements and New Communities

In 2008, Bishop Sam Jacobs, a long-time member of the Catholic Charismatic Renewal, invited national representatives of several movements to consider a possible collaboration on a national scale. Cursillo, Focolare, the Neocatechumenal Way, and Worldwide Marriage Encounter all immediately responded positively. Others joined the group over the years, participating in conference calls and personal meetings. This group was ultimately called, "Catholic Ecclesial Movements and New Communities in the U.S. in Conversation."

The following is a list of ecclesial movements and new communities who have participated in, or at least welcomed and encouraged efforts to communicate and collaborate on a national scale in union with Bishop Sam Jacobs and the U.S. episcopacy. Many of these groups have received approval or recognition by the Pontifical Council for the Laity; others have received approval or recognition by the local diocesan bishop in the U.S. All of them have Catholic membership. Each one seeks to radically implement the gospel in accordance with its founding inspiration. We are seeking contact with other movements and communities not included in this list.

- Alliance of Filipino Catholic Charismatic Prayer Communities – www.afccpc.org

- Apostolic Movement of Schoenstatt – www.schoenstatt.de/de/

- Arise International (Caritas in Veritate International) – www.caritasinveritate.com

- Beginning Experience International Ministry – www.beginningexperience.org

≈ Catholic Charismatic Renewal
  – www.nsc–chariscenter.org

≈ Catholic Engaged Encounter
  – www.engagedencounter.org/

≈ Catholic Fraternity of Charismatic Covenant Communities
  and Fellowships – www.catholicfraternity.net

≈ Christian Family Living – www.capemaymarianists.org

≈ Christian Family Movement – www.cfm.org

≈ Community of Sant'Egidio – www.santegidio.org

≈ Couples for Christ – www.couplesforchristusa.org/

≈ Emmanuel Community – www.emmanuelcommunity.com

≈ Focolare Movement – www.focolare.org/usa/en/

≈ Heart's Home – www.heartshomeusa.org

≈ International Federation of L'Arche Communities
  – www.larcheusa.org

≈ Le Conseil du Renouveau Charismatique Catolique des
  Haïtiens D'Outre–Mer – www.crccho.org

≈ Legion of Mary – www.legionofmary.com

≈ Life Teen – www.lifeteen.com

≈ Madonna House – www.madonnahouse.org

≈ Marriage Retorno – www.marriageretorno.org

≈ Movimiento Familiar Cristiano Catolico
  – www.mfccusa.net/

≈ National Christian Life Community of the USA
  – www.clc–usa.org

≈ National Cursillo Movement – www.cursillo.org

- Neocatechumenal Way
  – www.camminoneocatecumenale.it

- Pax Christi – www.paxchristiusa.org

- People of Praise Community– www.peopleofpraise.org

- Regnum Christi – www.regnumchristi.org/

- Renovación Carismática Católica Comité Nacional de Servicio Hispano – www.rcchispana.com

- Retrouvaille International – www.retrouvaille.org

- Teams of Our Lady – www.teamsofourlady.org

- TEC Conference – www.tecconference.org

- The Sword of the Spirit – www.swordofthespirit.net/

- Worldwide Marriage Encounter – www.wwme.org

The following six groups involved in the "Conversation" provided a brief description of their group.

Arise International
(Caritas in Veritate International)

A rise International, formerly known as Youth Arise International is a relational based international movement of young adults dedicated, through the grace of our own encounter with Christ, *to raising a generation of Leaders to be apostles of Charity and Truth for the mission of the Church.* Today, Arise International forms part of the Confederation Caritas in Veritate International.

Arise International:

> **relates** to various Pontifical dicasteries in the Vatican, such as *Cor Unum, Council for Laity, Council for the New Evangelization, Congregation of Faith and Propoganda Fidae.*

> **has as its vision** to raise a generation of leaders, men and women of God, committed husbands and wives, and parents, empowered by the Holy Spirit and open to the *Gospel of Life* and to equip students to reach out to other students with scientific and contemporary proofs of the existence of God.

> **is an expression of the spirituality of** *communion*, where individuals from varying countries, cultures, movements, and groups come together to be enriched through friendship (the sharing of their lives), mentoring (the sharing of their experiences), and collaboration (the sharing in common work apostolate). This *"communion"* expresses itself in the *"mission"* of the Church.[1]

---

1. At the threshold of the Third Millennium it is clear that the Church's ability to evangelize requires that she strive earnestly to serve the cause of unity in all its dimensions. Communion and mission go hand in hand. See *Novo Millennio Ineunte,* 24, John Paul II; see also 43.

is one founding movement behind *Caritas in Veritate International*, a confederation of 32 organizations for integral development and human progress at the direct service of the Holy Father. Its spirituality: Charity needs to be based on and incorporate the Truth, not a concept, nor a philosophy but a Person, the Son of God, Jesus.

was founded in 1994 in Malta; and through its partners today is present in all Europe, Asia, Africa, Latin America and USA.

For more information on mission trips and Leadership Forums contact:

Website: www.youtharise.org

Email: info@caritasinveritate.com.

Address: Arise International (Caritas in Veritate International)
3443 North Central Avenue, Suite 1405,
Phoenix, AZ 85012

Photo courtesy of Henry Cappello - President of Arise International (the youth section Caritas in Veritate International)

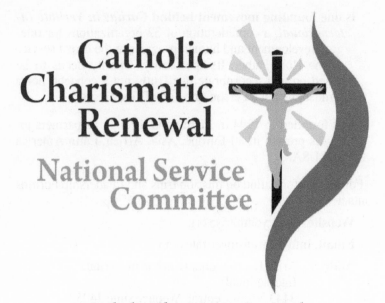

Catholic Charismatic Renewal
National Service Committee

Catholic Charismatic Renewal
National Service Committee

The Catholic Charismatic Renewal is a movement in the Catholic Church that began shortly after the Second Vatican Council. Its origins are usually dated to a retreat weekend held by several faculty members and students from Duquesne University in Pittsburgh, PA, in February 1967. At the retreat, the students sang the ancient hymn *Veni Creator Spiritus* and fervently prayed for God to deepen the grace of their baptism and confirmation. During the weekend many of the students experienced a powerful outpouring of the Spirit together with the gift of tongues, prophecy, and other charisms. This "Pentecost experience" quickly spread to other college campuses and continued to spread across the world, so that today the Catholic Charismatic Renewal exists in over 238 countries, having touched over 120 million Catholics.

There are between 2000 and 3000 mostly parish based prayer groups, and over a hundred branches of covenant communities encompassing several strands, some of which are gathered under the Catholic Fraternity of Covenant Communities and

Charismatic Fellowships which was established as an Association of Christ's Faithful in 1990. The International Catholic Charismatic Renewal Services (ICCRS) with offices in the Vatican was also recognized in 1993 as a Private Association of the Faithful. However, it has no juridical responsibility, only the service offered for the promotion of the Renewal.

In the U.S. there are various leadership groups; the oldest is the National Service Committee established in 1970. The others are the Association of Diocesan Liaisons encouraged into existence by the U.S. Bishops Ad Hoc Committee on the Catholic Charismatic Renewal in 1975; the Comité Nacional de Servicio Hispano, Le Conseil Du Renouveau Charismatique Catolique Des Haitiens D'Outre-Mer, and the Alliance of Filipino Catholic Charismatic Prayer Communities. In addition, the Renewal exists in the U.S. among Koreans, Portuguese, Indonesians, Vietnamese, and a number of other ethnic groups. It has been the Renewal's teaching and practice to be under the local ordinary in the Dioceses in which the Renewal exists.

The strongest dimension of the Renewal exists in Mexico, Central America, and South America. It is estimated that 65% of the active Renewal participants worldwide are from those regions. So too in the U.S., the strongest part of the Renewal today is among Hispanics.

At the heart of the Catholic Charismatic Renewal is the grace of baptism in the Holy Spirit which "is a life-transforming experience of the love of God the Father poured into one's heart by the Holy Spirit, received through a total surrender to the lordship of Jesus Christ." (*Baptism in the Holy Spirit*, p 9 published by ICCRS). This grace-event has many fruits not the least of which is openness to the charisms/gifts of the Holy Spirit which Pope Benedict XVI called "one of the positive elements and aspects of the Catholic Charismatic Renewal . . . and their merit lies in having recalled their topicality [importance] in the Church" (address October 31, 2008).

Pope Francis has indicated his support of the Renewal both by his actions and his words. As Archbishop of Buenos Aires he regularly met with Renewal leaders. Soon after his election as Pope he told the Italian Renewal: "Tell them that I love them very much...because I was responsible for the Charismatic Renewal in

Argentina, and that's why I love them very much." More recently Pope Francis spoke positively of the "prayer of praise" character-istic of the Renewal: "the prayer of praise is a Christian prayer for all of us" (address January 28, 2014). At the 37th Convocation of the Italian Renewal, in June, 2014, Pope Francis encouraged the Renewal with these words: "You, Charismatic Renewal, have received a great gift from the Lord.... Charismatic Renewal is a great force at the service of the proclamation of the Gospel, in the joy of the Holy Spirit.... I expect from you that you share with all, in the Church, the grace of Baptism in the Holy Spirit."

The Catholic Charismatic Renewal is at the service of the Church and the New Evangelization. It is, in the words of Cardinal Leon Suenens of Belgium, who was one of the more outspoken voices at the Second Vatican Council, "a movement of the Spirit offered to the entire Church and destined to rejuvenate every part of the Church's life."

For more information:

Website: www.nsc-chariscenter.org

Phone: 800–338–2445

Email: Chariscenter@nsc-chariscenter.org

The Cursillo Movement
Cursillos in Christianity

Mission Statement

To make a friend, be a friend, and bring our friends to Christ.

Vision Statement

To enable the person to be fully Christian, who in turn, will transform his/her environment to be more Christian by living his/her internal tripod of piety (heart), study (mind), and action (will).

The Spanish word Cursillo translates to "short course". What Cursillo offers is a short course in Christianity that lasts three days: Thursday evening through Sunday evening. When a person completes the short course (Cursillo), he/she is referred to as a Cursillista. There are approximately 1,000,000 Cursillistas in the United States and most every diocese offers Cursillo. The first Cursillo in Christianity weekend was held in August 1944 in Cala Figuera. Cursillo was introduced in the United States in 1957 in Waco, TX. Cursillos in Christianity received Canonical Recognition from the Pontifical Council for the Laity in May 2004.

The Cursillos in Christianity Movement originated in Palma de Majorca, Spain in the early 1940's. The Charism of Cursillo was given to the person of Eduardo Bonnín. Eduardo, the founder, believed that what the movement has achieved, all that it has tried to accomplish in the world, has become a reality because its author is the Holy Spirit. When the Charism of Cursillo was made known to the hierarchy in the 1940's, they blessed it with both hands as they witnessed its fruits in the person and the evangelization of environments.

Cursillos in Christianity is a worldwide lay ecclesial Movement. It was from this lay apostolate that the essence and purpose of Cursillo and the basis of its methodology originated after a thorough study of environments. In Cursillo, a lay path is designated because the strategy focuses on the person and the environments, rather than on structures. The essence of Cursillo is Jesus Christ and the reality of his love and friendship. The purpose of the Charism of Cursillo is directed to the person so that all women and men of the world will know the Good News that God in Christ loves them. The Cursillo methodology consists of three phases; Precursillo (before), Cursillo Weekend (during), and Postcursillo (after).

Each person that has experienced a Cursillo knows that to be Christian is to first feel being loved by God, and to live in awe of this reality, since what is most authentically Christian is to let God love us. The interior attitude created by this reality, when believed and lived fully, becomes a leaven and is transmitted to others. But, to grasp this, to experience it, to encounter God who is love, it is necessary to present ourselves to Him as we truly are.

The triple encounter, which takes place in the Cursillo: with oneself, with Christ, and with the brothers is in reality, becoming friends with oneself, with Christ, and with the brothers. This, together with loyalty to God's grace, offers the person criterion, which facilitates a more accurate orientation, the necessary light, and the constant courage to solve any problem according to God's light. Then, little by little, we understand that Christ has come to bring us true happiness, making the way simple and giving us the necessary means to become the true person he created.

Cursillos in Christianity weekends were born, not as a response from the Church to the world, but as a way to communicate to all men and women that that God loves each one. They were designed, structured, and prayed upon not to evangelize the world, but to evangelize the person. Cursillo came in order to awaken a hunger for God in the person and the world.

The purpose that Cursillo seeks is not for doing things but rather, for *being Christian* in the environment where God calls each person to serve. This life, through its encounter and friendship with Christ, is an inexhaustible source of effective evangelization in the family, neighborhood, workplace, leisure, and finally in the very space we occupy at this exact moment in our lives.

For more information:

Website: www.cursillo.org

Phone: 512-746-2020

Address: National Cursillo Movement
P.O. Box 799,
Jarrell, TX 76537

Focolare Movement (Work of Mary)

The Focolare Movement had humble beginnings in Trent, Italy, with a small group of young people gathered around Chiara Lubich, its foundress. During the horror and destruction of World War II, in which they experienced firsthand the vanity of all the things that they held dear, they made the simple-sounding but life-changing discovery that God is Love. While other young idealists were looking for brand new ideas and speaking about ideals upon which they would rebuild their lives and their land, Chiara and her friends chose God, God-Love, as their only Ideal. The only possession they carried with them into the air-raid shelters during the numerous bombardments was a small copy of the Gospels. The Gospel promises came alive for them as they lived out the words of Jesus in their daily lives, especially those concerning love of neighbor. Almost immediately a large community of people formed around this core group, people of all ages and walks of life, who wanted to share in this Gospel lifestyle. People began calling the small core group, "focolare" (Italian for "family hearth") because of the fire and the family warmth they felt when they were together with them, which they attributed to Jesus' promise to be among those who are united in his name, in his love (see Mt 18:20).

The Focolare Movement (Work of Mary) is an ecclesial movement approved by Pope John XXIII in 1962, present today in 182 nations. Subsequent Popes - Paul VI, John Paul II and Benedict XVI - repeatedly welcomed, affirmed and encouraged this new life precisely because it contributed so much to the Church's mission. Although it is most widespread in the Catholic Church, it is also found in 300 other churches and ecclesial communities and among the faithful of many other religions, as well as people of goodwill, who do not relate their lives directly to God.

The Focolare Movement's mission is all about unity - among individuals, groups, cities, and nations - to live and work for a united world according to Jesus' prayer to the Father "so that they may all be one, as you, Father, are in me and I in you" (Jn 17:21).

Its communitarian spirituality, known as the spirituality of unity, is a very appealing new way to live the Gospel for millions of people of all ages and backgrounds.

By living this spirituality all over the world, men, women, and children become seeds of a new people that promotes greater solidarity in humanity, especially with the poorest and the weakest. They introduce this spirit wherever they find themselves - in families, neighborhoods, parishes, schools, workplaces etc. While supporting and collaborating with other initiatives for harmony and unity, the Focolare offers a unique, sustaining spiritual resource based on the simple love of each particular neighbor in the present moment.

Lived not only by individual persons, but by small and large groups, the communitarian dimension of this spirituality is quite striking. Considering that the first community is the Church itself, Chiara Lubich always stressed unity with the hierarchy of the Church and with other Catholic groups and charisms. Inspired by these Christian principles, members of the Focolare do not disregard, but rather affirm, some of the same Gospel values which can be found in other faiths and cultures.

There are communities of the Focolare spread throughout the United States. In different cities, annual gatherings for members and friends of the movement are held, called the Mariapolis (City of Mary), where families, priests, religious, young people, and friends can come to experience and learn more about the movement and its spirituality. There is also a permanent Mariapolis, a little Focolare town, in Hyde Park, New York which welcomes visitors and holds periodic gatherings for Focolare members and friends throughout the year.

For more information:

Website: www.focolare.org/usa/en/

Email: webmaster@focolare.us

The Neocatechumenal Way

The Neocatechumenal Way is an *itinerary of Christian initiation*, initiated by Kiko Argüello and Carmen Hernandez during the years of the Second Vatican Council in the poorest slum of Madrid.

The situation of the Church today is similar to the one of the Early Church in the midst of paganism when people needed a Christian Initiation before baptism: the "catechumenate". Today, in a world ever more distant from Christianity and torn between secularization and fundamentalism, where many people have abandoned their faith and the Church, or live it at a very superficial level, it is necessary to rediscover what is the gift of divine life received in baptism.

Pope Paul VI, on May 8th, 1974, meeting with Kiko and Carmen said "...to promote this reawakening - is what you call a *'post-baptismal way'* which will be able to renew in today's Christian communities those effects of maturity...which in the early Church were obtained by the time of preparation to Baptism. ...*before or after Baptism is secondary. What matters is that you aim at the authenticity, at the fullness, at the consistency, at the sincerity of Christian life.* And this is a very great merit which consoles us immensely...."

Pope John Paul II, on August 30, 1990, in his letter *Ogni Qualvolta*, recognized the Neocatechumenal Way *"as an itinerary of catholic formation valid for our society and our time."* He expressed his desire that *"bishops may value and support"* this instrument for the New Evangelization *"so that it may be implemented according to the guidelines proposed by its initiators."*

Pope Benedict XVI, on January 12, 2006, met with members of the Neocatechumenal Communities and inaugurated a new form of evangelization sending 13 "Missio ad Gentes" in Northern Europe and North America. Each "Missio ad Gentes" is constituted by a presbyter, accompanied by four or five large families who, requested by a bishop, receive a mandate to evangelize dechristianized or pagan areas. These "Missio ad Gentes", following the "very first apostolic model", meet in the homes in the midst of non-baptized people. People who are far from the Church and pagans are coming back to the Church.

Pope Francis I, on February 1, 2014, meeting with about 12,000 members of the Neocatechumenal Way in order to send 450 families in mission and 42 new "Missio ad Gentes", said: *"...I thank the Lord for the joy of your faith and for the ardor of your Christian witness. Thanks be to God. ...My thoughts go out in a special way to the families who will go out to different parts of the world to proclaim and witness to the Gospel. The Church is grateful for your generosity!"*

Approval of final statutes

On June 13, 2008, five Congregations of the Holy See approved the final Statutes of the Neocatechumenal Way recognizing it as:

1. a post-baptismal catechumenate for people already baptized but who need to rediscover their baptism.

2. a catechumenate for non-baptized people, as a concrete way for implementing the RCIA (Rite of Christian Initiation of Adults).

"The recent approval of the Statutes of the Way *has sealed the esteem and benevolence with which the Holy See follows the work that the Lord has inspired through your Initiators.* The Pope, Bishop of Rome, thanks you for the generous service you offer to the evangelization of this City and for the dedication with which you work to bring the Christian proclamation into every environment" (Pope Benedict XVI on January 10, 2009). On that occasion the Holy Father inaugurated a new form of mission: *communitates in missione* — sending communities who have already finished their itinerary of Christian initiation, to help parishes in difficult areas of Rome.

Approval of "Catechetical Directory"

On January 17, 2011, after receiving the mandate from the Congregation for the Doctrine of the Faith, the Pontifical Council for the Laity decreed that, "following a thorough doctrinal study of the matter", the catechesis of the Way... now become the *"Catechetical Directory of the Neocatechumenal Way."*

"With these ecclesial seals" - Pope Benedict said - *"the Lord confirms and entrusts to you anew this precious instrument – which is the Way—so that you may [...] contribute, with new impetus and ardor, to the radical and joyful rediscovery of the gift of baptism and to offer your original contribution to the cause of the New Evangelization. The Church has recognized in the Neocatechumenal Way a particular gift aroused by the Holy Spirit."*

Redemptoris Mater Seminaries

Since the beginning, the Neocatechumenal communities have participated in great numbers to the World Youth Days and thousands of youth have offered themselves for priesthood or religious life. The flourishing of numerous vocations led Pope John Paul II in 1987 to open a Diocesan Missionary Seminary in Rome, the *Redemptoris Mater*, to assist many dioceses worldwide which have scarcity of priests. His example was followed by many bishops so that today 100 *Redemptoris Mater Seminaries* have been erected worldwide. Around 2,000 priests have already been ordained and 2,000 seminarians are preparing for priesthood.

Data

Today there are more than 20,000 communities in 6,000 parishes that are part of 800 dioceses spread over 120 nations. In the United States there are about 1,000 communities in 80 dioceses and there are 8 *Redemptoris Mater Seminaries* located in the following dioceses: Newark, Denver, Washington, Boston, Dallas, Miami, Philadelphia and Guam.

For more information:

Website: www.camminoneocatecumenale.it

Email: neocatechumenalway@gmail.com

Worldwide Marriage Encounter

Our Vision

"Love one another as I have loved you." Jn 15:12

Our Mission

The Mission of Worldwide Marriage Encounter is to proclaim the value of Marriage and Holy Orders in the Church and in the world.

Our Charism

Faith through Relationship

Worldwide Marriage Encounter is the largest pro-marriage movement in the world! It deepens the joys of married couples who desires a richer life together and provides support and encouragement to priests in their vocation.

The message of Worldwide Marriage Encounter is simple: "Love one another as I have loved you." Over the past 46 years, inspired by the passion and dreams of Fr. Chuck Gallagher, SJ, and thousands of dedicated couples and priests, this Vision has helped our Movement spread to almost 100 countries. Fr. Chuck envisioned the Weekend as not only a vehicle to enrich marriages, but to renew our Church by revitalizing the Sacraments of Marriage and Holy Orders. We witness the Good News in a powerful way by embracing our mission: "to proclaim the value of Marriage and Holy Orders in the Church and in the world."

The foundation of our Movement is the Worldwide Marriage Encounter Weekend, presented by a team of couples and a priest who share deeply about their own relationships. Participants are offered practical concepts and tools to honor their marriage vows and nurture life-giving relationships. Through dialogue, they learn a different way of communicating that leads to greater intimacy. Married couples come to see God's desire for them is unity - one man and one woman made in the image of God. They experience a new awareness of their Sacrament of Marriage as a sign of God's love and are urged to share that love with our Church and the world.

Living the charism of Worldwide Marriage Encounter – Faith through Relationship - leads to renewal in the Church and change in the world through these key elements:

- Ecumenism—Worldwide Marriage Encounter is Roman Catholic in expression but is open to all married couples regardless of their faith. The Weekend experience has also been adapted by many other faith expressions, inviting people of each faith tradition to live the concepts according to their beliefs.

- Relationship—Central to Worldwide Marriage Encounter is open, honest, tender, and trusting relationships - between husband and wife, couples and priests, priests and their communities, and each person's relationship with God.

- Spirituality—In living the concepts of the Worldwide Marriage Encounter Weekend, many participants discover the beauty of their vocation for the first time, making their sacraments come alive! Couples recognize God's desires for their relationship and priests are called into greater communion with their people. They are empowered to become witnesses of God's love!

- Evangelization—This new awareness of their Sacrament calls couples to reflect God's love more clearly to their children and to become beacons of light in the parish community. Their relationship is the foundation of the family and their home becomes a model of the Domestic Church. Couples become Good News for others as they participate in the evangelizing mission of the greater Church.

- A dialoguing lifestyle—The dialogue process learned on the Weekend leads to belonging and unity. Daily dialogue helps husbands and wives communicate deeply through life's challenges and encourages priests to build life-giving relationships while being more accessible to those they serve.

- Community—Worldwide Marriage Encounter leads to the growth of a community offering continuing support. Couples and priests meet regularly to share their faith and explore topics related to marriage and family. This local community is a real experience of Church, living out Christ's call to "Love one another as I have loved you."

- Co-responsibility of Couples and Priests—As couples and priests proclaim the gospel through their Sacraments of Marriage and Holy Orders, they create a vital model of "inter-sacramentality" for our Church, with leadership teams comprised of a couple and priest journeying together as an "ecclesial team."

In an age when the sanctity and value of Marriage and Priesthood are challenged on a daily basis, we give thanks to the Holy Spirit for inspiring this beautiful, life-changing Worldwide Marriage Encounter movement!

For more information:

Website: www.wwme.org

Phone: 909–863–9963

Email: wwmeoffice@sbcglobal.net

Acknowledgments

First Edition

I would like to acknowledge with gratitude the great work of all at New City Press, in particular Gary Brandl for his constant encouragement along the way, Tom Masters for his very careful editing work and Julie James for her diligence in marketing. There are many others, family and friends, colleagues, students of St. Patrick's College, Maynooth, as well as members of movements who have influenced my thinking behind this work. In particular, members of the Focolare Movement. I am indebted to them all. While all errors are mine, I am grateful to those who read initial drafts and provided valuable comments, especially Maire O'Byrne, David Hickey and Michael Mullaney.

Second Edition

New City Press would like to thank Maria Dalgarno for her outstanding editing and writing for the Abridged Second Edition. References, endnotes, and bibliography that may apply to this Abridged Second Edition can be found in detail in the First Edition.

NEW CITY PRESS
of the Focolare
Hyde Park, New York

New City Press is one of more than 20 publishing houses sponsored by the Focolare, a movement founded by Chiara Lubich to help bring about the realization of Jesus' prayer: "That all may be one" (John 17:21). In view of that goal, New City Press publishes books and resources that enrich the lives of people and help all to strive toward the unity of the entire human family. We are a member of the Association of Catholic Publishers.

Further Reading—Books by New City Press

Books by Fr. Brendan Leahy
Marian Profile	978-1-56548-139-8	$14.95
Priests Today	978-1-56548-346-0	$9.95
Believe in Love	978-1-56548-421-4	$13.95
His Mass and Ours	978-1-56548-448-1	$7.95
Going to God Together	978-1-56548-483-2	$11.95
Ecclesial Movements and Communities		
(Unabridged First Edition)	978-1-56548-395-5	$16.95

Periodicals
Living City Magazine,
www.livingcitymagazine.com

Scan to join our mailing list for discounts and promotions

or go to

www.newcitypress.com

and click on "join our email list."